"Why do you want to write a book about your life?" I was asked by a friend many years ago when the idea began to grow in my mind. "You haven't done anything spectacular, you aren't a famous politician, a noted actor, or a media personality. Who would want to know about your life?"

These are legitimate questions that deserve a response. During the last two years, with the help of a professional biographer who prepares memoirs for others, I have chronicled highlights of more than sixty years on this small planet, and I am satisfied with the book that now is in your hands.

Our Four Loaves of Bread is designed to be a tutorial rather than an entertainment medium, although it may include entertaining anecdotes. What I have accomplished since the 1930s when I began my trek through life on a small farm north of Manila, can be accomplished by others, and that is the purpose of the book.

If Rufino could do it, others can do it, is the message I wish to leave with readers, particularly with the younger generations of men and women who have so much life ahead of them.

If Rufino could survive some very bleak years as a child during the World War II atrocities by our captors, others can survive their temporary bleak years through whatever physical, mental, and poverty conditions may dominate their current situations.

If Rufino could seek out and complete his education to include seminary training and a bachelor of science degree in education, others can resolve to educate themselves out of what may seem to be a dark and pathetic beginning to life.

If Rufino could set and achieve specific goals throughout his life, others can do the same. Those who have no goals, no matter how small, float through the years without direction. As a consequence, they don't command their destiny; they simply exist. In a parallel sense, those who accept the use of illegal drugs as a way of life, no longer own their life; they just inhabit a warm body that has been taken over by their drug dealer.

If Rufino could time and again work his way through serious physical and mental situations and emerge the victor, others can overcome what may seem to be their most maddening physical and mental situations.

Many of us grow to recognize the delicious help that God is willing to give us when we recognize his presence and mercy. One of the most powerful and comforting phrases for me is

"Dear God, help me; guide me through this crisis because I honestly don't know what to do."

If Rufino could have the great fortune of courting and marrying a most wonderful partner who brought four loaves of bread into this world and who has remained steadfastly loyal to her husband through both joyous and difficult situations, then others can learn that marriage is not a convenient stopover to satisfy lust and convenience but, rather, a heady adventure that often requires the merging of two distinct opinions, two diverse desires, and two strong convictions into one course of action. I would not be the individual I am today without the loving presence of Eppie in my daily life.

This is not a tutorial in the sense that it contains an outline, propositions, examples, and a summary of what has been accomplished. Indeed, much of what I wish readers to understand about my life will never be transparent. Like an aroma of warm bread, the *sense* rather than the *facts* will drift into the reader's subconsciousness to be used, or not, by unconscious selection.

On the whole, I believe I have lived, and continue to live, the kind of life that God intends for us to embrace. Our days from birth to death are supremely short when compared to what is ahead for us in eternity. Whatever our religion, we must come to grip with what lies ahead of us. For some, that answer, unfortunately, is nothing. Those of us who believe in God have choices to make throughout our life that will determine whether we spend eternity in the presence of God or away from the warmth of his presence.

A good baker prepares for today and plans carefully for tomorrow. Eppie and I have guided the development of our four loaves of bread to give us confidence that they also will become bakers after us and produce their own loaves of bread as the endless cycle of life brings forth generation after generation of God's favored creatures. When we are called home for eternal rest, we can be assured that we have left a path of activity and guidance that will provide the incentive for other bakers to make this a better world than we found it.

God gave us the gift of life; what we do with our life is our gift back to him.

Our Four Loaves of Bread

Rufino S. Licos

Copyright © 2004 by Rufino S. Licos

Cover design by Molly Quirk.

ISBN 0-7414-1900-9

Published by:
INFINITY
PUBLISHING.COM
519 West Lancaster Avenue
Haverford, PA 19041-1413
Info@buybooksontheweb.com
www.buybooksontheweb.com
Toll-free (877) BUY BOOK
Local Phone (610) 520-2500
Fax (610) 519-0261

Printed in the United States of America

Printed on Recycled Paper

Published February 2004

Acknowledgments

Preparation of this book has taken many willing hands from beginning to end. I thank each of you for adding to my memories and the recounting of my fulfilling life.

I especially acknowledge the tremendous aid and comfort given to me by Eppie, my wonderful wife and cherished companion, who has been at my side for twenty-eight challenging years. Without her, I would not have been instrumental in bringing our four wonderful daughters (our loaves of bread) into our lives, nor would I have experienced the excitement of life that Eppie continuously pushes upon me with a quiet yet steady cherishing and caring that only a couple truly in love can understand and appreciate.

Heidi, Gina, Neri, and Raechel Licos

Our daughters have been the leading loves of our lives, and I thank each of them – Heidi, Regina (Gina), Neri, and Raechel – for maturing so well from infancy to adulthood while retaining a strong bond among the family.

I acknowledge the lengthy and diligent help given to me by J. Bryant VanCronkhite, who appeared to me out of the air when I needed help in turning scribbled words into the coherent pages of this book, and who worked with me for almost two years in the writing and publishing of *Our Four Loaves of Bread.*

My deep thanks also to Molly Quirk who designed and prepared the artistic covers.

Most importantly, I gratefully acknowledge the grace of God who directed me to prepare this book as a guide for young men and women in every country as they focus on their inheritance of the world and their role in its salvation for his sake.

Dedication

This book is dedicated to all the young men and women in the Philippines who gaze into the beautiful hills of our beloved country and dream of a land thousands of miles away. I, too, dreamed of such a land years ago, and my dream became reality when I arrived in the United States of America.

I never forgot my roots and I frequently return to my homeland — often with my family — to visit family and friends and to take part in treasured Filipino rites and events.

The events of my life that I describe on the following pages are intended to help young people in both countries prepare themselves for a life of learning, sharing, and giving. True happiness, I have learned, comes from continuous learning and then using that learning and experience to help others. The God of Christians, Jews, and Muslims expects us to put the welfare of others at least on the same level as our own welfare. When we honor God and truly attempt to live by His laws, He will see to it that our basic needs are met as we journey through this brief period on earth before joining him in heaven.

There is great turmoil now among some elements of Christians and Muslims, each of whom plays an important role in securing a healthy future for the Philippines. Yet both sects can live in harmony as long as their followers are willing to recognize the right of each group to select and honor their own religious beliefs.

Our future as a nation and a culture depends upon our young people and how they visualize their role on our planet. My role has been to help others through education and compassion. I recommend the same course to my readers.

May God bless each of you and watch over you daily.

Rufino S. Licos

Foreword
Thuy Pham-Remmele

During the winter of 2002, while I was coordinating the Lunar New Year Celebrations for Madison Asian Communities, I had the great fortune to develop a friendship with Rufino when we observed rare traditional Filipino dances performed by him, his graceful wife, and his lovely daughter Raechel.

At our 2003 Whitewater Faculty Spring Fling, Rufino amazed our guests with his agility and grace, charming everyone as he conducted an impromptu dance class.

A valuable Vietnamese saying declares that one must know a person not just by name and appearance, but through deeds that truly reveal the heart and character. For decades, Rufino has been a patient teacher, a loving husband, a proud father, and a dedicated chef who reigns in his kitchen and cooks for family and friends with pride and love. (Eppie confides that during twenty-eight years of marriage, she has not yet cooked a serious meal.)

As a caring friend should be, Rufino is ever ready with a helping hand. "Call me anytime!" are his famous parting words, and he truly means his continuing offer to help others.

Rufino is a humble artist who represents the best characteristics often linked to Filipinos. He knows how to live, and on Life's canvas he paints the most beautiful masterpieces in everyday interactions. To know him is to love him as he enriches us with his gentle soul and his contagious love of life.

Madison, Wisconsin
December 2003

Preface

Princess Emraida Kiram
Philippines

When Rufino Licos emigrated to America in 1968, like many Filipinos of that era, he left his homeland to take advantage of greater professional opportunities and the desire to build a brighter future for himself, his future wife, and whatever children they might bring into the world.

Because there were few Filipinos in the United States, compared with the Filipino population today, and no supporting family structures, those years were fraught with homesickness, loneliness, and sacrifices for many. But there was an indomitable spirit within the emigres that prodded them silently to persevere because failure was not an option for them.

Many Filipinos now have secured enviable reputations for themselves and have become role models for others to observe and copy. We constantly are amazed at what we can do given the right opportunity and support. Filipinos are distinguishing themselves in numerous professions, thereby returning spiritual, cultural, and financial blessings to their communities and churches.

Most of all, they take care of other Filipinos. Their cultural traditions have served them well.

Filipinos live in all states within the United States today as well as in several countries around the world as a result of substantially more employment opportunities. An estimated seven million Filipinos are employed worldwide as *overseas Filipino workers* (OFW). These OFW's have made globalization a household word.

The funds they return to their extended families back home help measurably to support countless families, educate children and relatives, provide the means for others to purchase luxury goods, and improve the daily lives of Filipinos throughout the Islands. Some of these funds were invested in small-scale businesses that made it possible for the Philippine economy to survive the Asian stock market crash in the late 1990's and continue to prop up the country's deteriorating economy.

When American Filipinos return home for visits, they generally are able to take their Island families on vacations, present them with opportunities to visit tourist spots within their country, enjoy brief visits at luxury hotels, and purchase the latest gadgets – opportunities many families never even dreamed possible.

OFW's often are highly educated individuals, yet willing to accept menial jobs or employment because any work abroad is better than what is available in their homeland. Living abroad has made most of us vocal advocates for changes in our beloved country. Through intense lobbying we have achieved voting privileges, a right denied us for so long.

OFW's most likely will impact the next national elections, not only with our votes but with our ability to influence voters and friends within our circles back home. We have come together to begin the process of opening banks, mortgage companies, real estate companies, hotels, and other businesses that will serve the needs of those remaining on the Islands.

We offer programs that provide scholarships and business entrepreneurship to families in the Philippines, because we can no longer wait for the government to meet these necessities.

Men and women like Rufino and Eppie Licos symbolize the new heroes of the Filipino culture. More nationalistic now than we were before we left the Philippines, we see ourselves as the salvation of the next generation. While the Filipinos distinguished ourselves with "people power" when we worked together to oust two corrupt presidents by marching *en masse* on the streets, true people power lies within the hearts of all the young men and women who will shed tears of loneliness yet will waken the next morning to continue the fight to save their country from the cancer that lurks within.

The paradigms have changed but the spirit that ennobled these people remains the same. Hope springs eternal. One day, we will see the Philippines regenerated from the sweat of its citizens bringing reforms from *without* because we know it will never happen from *within*. To those before and those coming next, may Allah bless us all.

Milwaukee, Wisconsin
December 2003

Chapters of My Life

Chapter 1 - Page 9. California – The early years in the Philippines; the seminary years, teaching at St. Louis University; my decision to live in America; the trip to California, stopovers in Tokyo at night and Hawaii in the sun.

Chapter 2 - Page 38. Getting Started – A brief stay north of Los Angeles; roadside lunch food; helping to build a house.

Chapter 3 - Page 46. Richland Center – the wonders of American high schools; experiencing snow; renewing my dancing abilities; working with AFS students and Boy Scouts; lessons in democracy; eating my way through eggs; simplifying mathematics.

Chapter 4 - Page 67. Waterloo – moving west to attend the University finding another great high school; more student travel; dancing through life; off to Spain; Citizen Licos; Dad comes to America.

Chapter 5 - Page 85. Romance – Eppie and I become partners for life.

Chapter 6 - Page 97. Madison – our "four loaves of bread" begin to arrive; a terrible accident for me and then for Eppie; life as a waiter, drug store clerk, clothing salesman, and airport security officer; becoming Senator Nelson's "son"; Antonia Yecla; the Schoenstatt Movement; Grampas' Nick and Earl.

Chapter 7 - Page 125. Homecoming – Our wonderful children earn silver crowns and white sashes as queens of several competitions.

Chapter 8 - Page 141. Joys of Living – Our friends and colleagues reflect on the Licos family.

Chapter 1: The Journey Begins

My eyes were blinded by the bright rays of the sun as I looked over my left shoulder and waved my right hand at the crowd. I searched for the faces of my parents, brothers, relatives, and friends who had accompanied me to the airport.. Thankfully, the heat of the early morning sun was tempered by the cold breeze common to the month of July in the Philippines.

In my left hand, I carried the only piece of luggage I owned. How many others were leaving their native country this morning, I wondered, and were they, like me, carrying with them all their possessions – two sets of underwear, one dress shirt, one pair of pants, two T-shirts, and a few handkerchiefs?

My throat became tight with tension as I approached the waiting airplane. Each stride seemed to become shorter as though some inner being was trying to persuade me to not board the aircraft and leave my native land of twenty-seven years.

Would I ever see my mother and father again? What would happen to me in making the transition from the Philippines to the United States of America? Was this a foolish move on my part? Was there still time to turn around and race back to the only family I knew?

Taking a last look at family
and friends, MIA, 1968

I was certain my eyes were red with stress and tears I was holding back as I continued to search for my loved ones through the glass walk that separated me from my family. I waved again as I saw my mother wiping tears from her eyes.

My brothers and friends were covering first the left and then the right side of their eyes with their hands to focus more closely on me as I mounted the aircraft stairs.

That first step was monumental in my mind. One step up, carrying me, perhaps forever, away from my wonderful islands. One step up, carrying me to my destiny thousands of miles from home. There was no return now. Today was July 21, 1968.

I squared my shoulders, resisted a final opportunity to turn and run, and boarded the JAL four-engine plane that was to carry me to my first stopover in Japan. As I walked toward seat F-13 on the left side of the plane, I realized that my heart was beating faster. A giant wave of great fear surged through my body. My hands shook as I shifted to gain a better view through the window.

Crewmen were checking the plane's exterior. Two men on the left side were filling the gas tanks. Another was occupied with the electrical convertors. One crewman wearing head-

Licos family (dad and mom at left) with Rufino at Manila Airport on departure day on July 21, 1968

phones was signaling to the pilot in the cockpit as well as other crew members on the ground.

A young stewardess with a beautiful smile on her face walked along the aisle, greeting each passenger and checking the overhead compartments where passengers stored hand-carries. When she arrived at the front of the passenger compartment, she reached for an oxygen mask and explained its use. The thought of needing to breathe into an oxygen mask didn't relieve me of my built-up anxiety. My heart pounded louder and stronger.

I clasped my hands in my lap and prayed to God, the remaining stable force in my life at the moment, while the plane sped down the runway. Moments later, I dared to look out the window. Not too far below, I saw buildings and then, suddenly, the ocean. We were leaving my country. For some reason, I smiled and told myself, today is perfect for traveling.

Several minutes passed before the stewardess announced that we might unfasten our seat belts since we were now three thousand feet above the water.

A second stewardess came down the aisle pushing a cart stacked high with a variety of soft drinks. When she asked what I would prefer to drink, I wasn't certain how to answer. The man sitting beside me asked for a *Coke*. I decided to play it safe.

Rufino and former student, Mario de la Peña, branch manager of a La Union bank.

"A Coke, please."

Passengers began to stand, stretch, and visit the rest rooms. I settled into my seat and turned my thoughts to my mom, dad, brothers, relatives, and friends who brought me to the airport. A stewardess walked down the aisle, distributing headphones to each passenger, even though I didn't know what to do with it. My seat companion kindly showed me how to plug it into a jack on the seat ahead of me so I could hear music.

I pretended to listen to the music, but my mind was occupied with many other matters. What shall I do when I get to America? Where shall I stay? Who shall I contact? Since I told no one that I was coming to America, how would I find them in that vast land?

11

I didn't even know where my uncle lived, but I thought it was somewhere in the state of California. I should have written him to let him know I was coming to the United States.

Maryhurst Seminary students-1968

* * * *

My mind raced back through the last five years when I taught at St. Louis University in the area known as the gateway to the Cordillera Mountain Range that transverses the Montanosa mountain, home of many indigenous tribes.

The University opened in 1911 as a one-room elementary school for ten local boys. It grew into a high school by 1921 and took on college level courses in 1952. University status was bestowed in 1963. There currently are twenty-three buildings and about 25,000 students.

It was only a few months ago that I read in the paper that an American recruiter was in Manila interviewing teachers for positions in the United States. I left for the city on Friday night and found hundreds of teachers lined up to crowd into a small room at the Manila Hotel.

I was fortunate to meet and be interviewed by a Mr. Bair. A tape recorder was placed at the center of the table between us to record all the questions and answers. These interviews were sent to schools in the United States where students listened to determine if they could understand our accents when we spoke in English.

Rufino (front) and friends in Hundred Islands, Philippines.

One month later, in April, 1967, I received a letter from Mr. Bair informing me that I passed the interview and could begin to apply for an emigration visa. I completed the paperwork to emigrate to the United States but took no further action to continue the process.

Should I move to America or remain in this country? This was one of the most demanding decisions in my life. I loved teaching at Baguio. The students made me feel very important because of my skills. In addition to teaching at St. Louis in the afternoon, I taught at Maryhurst Seminary in the morning.

When my students in the seminary got wind that I might leave for the United States, they took me to see the movie *To Sir with Love*. The following Monday, we discussed the movie in class since I was teaching English literature then.

"Mr. Licos, what did you think of the movie?"

"I really enjoyed it."

"We hope you consider the choice of Sidney Portier at the end of the movie."

Sidney Portier was a teacher in that movie who tore up a contract that offered him a better job. My students at St. Louis and the seminary were hoping I would follow Sidney's decision and remain in the Philippines. I replied that I was going to try to enter the United States. If I failed, I added, I would be back to teach them again.

On the very last day of school, they prepared a memory book expressing their gratitude for having me as their teacher and friend. It was a heartbreaking moment.

I traveled from the province to the city of Manila to go for my interview and for my physical exam. At Singian Clinic where I had my physical exam, an unusual incident took place. Five of us, all young men, were waiting for the results of our X-ray that would determine if we had tuberculosis or any other health problem. Any evidence of that disease would keep us out of the United States.

An older lady sitting across me smiled and spoke to me.

"You are such a very lucky young man," she said..

"Well, thank you. Why do you say that?"I replied.

"Let me see your palm," she continued. "See here, look at these lines. You indeed are a very lucky man. Wherever you go or whatever your plans may be in the future, you will always be successful in life. People will love you."

I smiled and thanked her. A moment later, my name was called by a nurse. The other four men wished me good luck.

My heart started to beat faster and I felt quite nervous. I was convinced I would receive bad news from the nurse since, at only ninety-eight pounds, I was the smallest and thinnest of the five men.

"The results of your X-ray and physical exams came in," the doctor said slowly. He was not smiling and my heart sank. Here comes the bad news, I said to myself.

"Mr. Licos," the doctor said with a smile coming across his face, "congratulations, you passed the physical exam. You will be allowed to emigrate to the United States."

I almost toppled over when I heard him speak that last line. I raised my eyes and thanked God.

"Bring these papers and your X-ray film to the embassy and file for your passport and visa," the doctor continued.

"The other men?" I asked. "Will they be allowed to emigrate to the United States?"

The doctor looked at me with a sad face.

"Not to the United States, I'm sorry to say. None of them passed the physical exam."

My knees were still shaking as I left the clinic.

* * * *

"In a few minutes we will serve dinner," the flight attendant announced. "If you want to use the restroom, this would be a good opportunity to do so."

The other two attendants passed out food trays on both aisles. I unfolded the small table that was built into the seat ahead of me, closed my eyes, and continued listening to the soft and calming music.

Promoting condensed millk.

"Do you care for a drink, with your dinner, sir?"

The attendant startled me. I sat bolt upright. She smiled, understanding my confusion. How many young Filipinos had received their first flight tray from her over the years. She waited patiently for my reply, smiling kindly at me.

"A small glass of wine, Miss, please," I managed to reply, trying to act like a seasoned traveler. The wine appeared immediately, followed soon by a delicious supper of rice, a vegetable, chicken, and salad. A small cup of fruit cocktail completed the meal.

"May I have a *Pepsi* or a *Coke*, please," I asked when the youthful attendant reappeared. She smiled that reassuring smile and poured a *Coke* into a small plastic glass. I accepted it like the seasoned traveler I had become in the space of a few hours. What a life! Flying was not so bad and scary after all.

In a short time, the attendant came along to collect the dinner trays.

"Is there anything you need, sir?" she asked.

"A deck of playing cards, please," I directed with growing strength in my voice. After all, I was a veteran traveler now. The attendant produced a deck of cards. I played solitaire for about an hour and then felt my eyes become tired, calling for a rest. I reached up over my head, turned off the light above me, lowered the volume of the music coming over my headset, closed my eyes, and reflected on the last few days.

My thoughts turned to what would happen when I reached California? What should I do when I arrive at the airport?

Where would I be able to get help? I had heard that people in America are kind and helpful. If my uncles came to America in 1926 without any formal education, would I be able to survive as a young, educated man?

God will provide everything as long as I continue to have faith in Him, I said firmly just before I dozed off.

Stopover Tokyo

Please return to your seats and fasten your seatbelts, the stewardess announced over the speakers. "If your tables are down, put them up at this time. In fifteen to twenty minutes we will be landing at Osaka Airport in Japan. We are experiencing some engine problem; everything is under control, but please stay in your seat."

The plane gave a great jerk and I started to get nervous again. The man next to me turned said: "Don't worry, we're just going through some air pockets. That's the reason we experience sudden jerks once in awhile."

15

I asked myself, what are air pockets? Now I was really scared and I held my pillow extra tightly as I looked through the window. Not too far beneath the plane I saw the ocean and buildings along the shore.

Again, the stewardess spoke: "In a few minutes, we will land in Osaka. Please stay in your seat when we're on the ground and wait for further instructions."

Everyone remained seated quietly. Most of the passengers were Filipinos. Some were businessmen and others, like me, were emigrating to the United States. Their faces showed signs of worry, just as I"m certain mine did.

The plane began to descend. The waiting seemed longer than the flight itself. As we approached the airport, my heart seemed to beat faster and faster. I felt warm all over my body. Perspiration rolled down my forehead. I held my breath, waiting for just what to happen I really didn't know. There was a slight bump and I felt the tires of the plane touch the runway. I breathed out again and sank back into the comfort of my seat. Everyone seemed relieved as the plane came to a halt.

"Please stay in your seats and wait for further instructions," the stewardess reminded us in a calm and friendly tone that made us all feel more comfortable. "You may unfasten your seat belts now."

Five minutes later, a male voice came over the speaker system with a tone of authority.

"Ladies and gentlemen, this is your captain speaking. Due to an engine problem, we will transfer to another airplane for the trip to Tokyo, where we will spend the night. Therefore, please take your hand carry luggage and any other possessions with you when you leave the airplane.

"It is now about 4:30 in the afternoon. We will leave on the other plane at approximately 5:00 p.m. Thank you, and I am sorry for any inconvenience."

I carried my traveling bag in my right hand. In my left hand was my large brown envelope containing my X-ray negative that I needed to show to the immigration officers in Hawaii. When we were settled on the other plane, the stewardess spoke again.

"The flight from here to Tokyo is about 90 minutes long. As soon as we land, please take all your belongings and proceed to Gate 6. A bus will be there to take you to the hotel where you will spend your evening. Enjoy your flight; we'll see you tomorrow morning."

16

The trip to Tokyo was uneventful. When the city came into view after dark, I looked through the window and watched the "heavens" down below with its beautiful, sparkling lights. I had never seen anything so massive and awesome.

As the plane approached the airport, my heart pounded both with apprehension and an-ticipation. My eyes immediately took in the lights of Tokyo, but my brain took its time to adjust to this phenome-non. The rows of lights that illuminated the streets, bolstered by the bright lights of the buildings, made the city look like the heavens.

The Licos family, 1968; brothers Artemio and Florendo standing; Father, Rufino, Mother sittting

The plane came to a halt and we all sighed with relief. I took my hand-carry and led the way to Gate 6. We boarded the waiting bus that took us to the front of the large Honeda Hotel. Mauro, another passenger, introduced himself and asked me if this was my first trip overseas. He was a businessman from Ilocos Norte who traveled between the Philippines and the United State twice a year.

Mauro and I spoke the same dialect. He was kind enough to accompany me to the desk, where I registered and received my room key. The female Japanese clerk told me I would be in room 1603. That meant I was on the 16th floor. She pointed to the elevator and told me to call the desk if I needed anything. Mauro bade me a good night and said: "I'll see you tomorrow. The worker at the front desk will waken us in the morning."

I pushed the button pointing up and waited for a man and woman who had been on the airplane. The woman asked me my room number. I told them 1603 and she responded that she and her husband would be in 1602. We entered the elevator and faced the door. I learned that the couple were from Tarlac and were traveling to San Francisco. The door of the elevator opened and the three of us got out. We walked a few doors to the left and I saw that their room was just across from mine.

I opened my door, switched on the light, and was surprised to see such a huge room all for myself. The bed was far too large for a man my size. There also was a television set in the room, and a telephone on a night stand. Recovering from my initial shock, I set my bag on the floor and my large X-ray envelope on the bed. Further exploration revealed a large bathroom that contained a magnificent vanity set, a toilet, and a bathtub.

Returning to my bed, I attempted to turn on the television set but it didn't seem to work. Leaving it alone for later examination, I pulled the string of the curtain in front of the large window. The curtain opened, revealing a fantastic display of dazzling lights in every direction. What a beautiful sight. I still can't come up with the words to describe Tokyo at night. My eyes feasted on the sights of the city for twenty minutes.

At last, I picked up the receiver of the phone and called the desk for assistance. Five minutes passed and then I heard a knock at the door. A Japanese man stood in front of my door. I asked him to turn on the television set and show me how to use the shower. He was a very polite young man who bowed each time he spoke.

After a wonderful, warm shower, I went to bed. Watching television from the bed was an inviting concept, but I turned it off after a few minutes since most of the channels were in the Japanese language. I could hardly go to sleep. I closed my eyes, but my mind was occupied with an unending list of questions. How were my parents, relatives, and friends who I left behind? What should I do when I get to California? How eventful will our flight from Tokyo to Hawaii be? Will our entrance to the United States through customs in Hawaii go smoothly?

*   *   *   *   *

I was carefully hidden behind a large pillow tucked in the corner of the house. I didn't know where Florendo and Artemio were hiding. I could see Mother lying on a table in the kitchen, surrounded by laughing Japanese soldiers. They were forcing her to drink water from a water sprinkler. Each time she could drink no more, they stepped on her stomach until the water was propelled onto the ground from her mouth.

I wanted to run to Mother and scream at the Japanese soldiers to stop torturing her, but she had impressed upon me that a four-year-old boy had no power over the invaders during World War II, and I must have no contact at all with them. It was a terrible sight for me to see as a small boy, and a terrible experience for my mom.

Dad was the Barrio Capitan of our village. He and the other men hid in the middle of our sugar cane plantation when the Japanese soldiers were in the area. The men knew it was useless to fight in direct combat, so they hid and then used their survival skills to take care of their families as best they could.

The Japanese soldiers used our backyard to torture both Filipino and American soldiers. Mom began to hide me behind the pillow after the soldiers became cruel to children. Despite the torture, Mom never let on that she and Dad were hiding ten American soldiers on our land. They had dug a hole where the Americans lay silently when the soldiers came near. Mom fed them once a day for several days. I never knew what happened to the American soldiers.

Saint Louis University
college graduate - 1963

19

First class as a teacher; 1963
at Antamok Tram.

One night my dad evacuated the entire family to a mountain some twenty-five miles from our home. There we learned survival techniques. On top of the mountain, we could see American and Japanese planes maneuvering in dog fights. When I returned to my home in 1945, American soldiers were camped throughout the area. They gave us chocolate bars and I learned how to greet them. "Hi, Joe," I would say, and they would give me a chocolate bar and treat me like a little brother.

My dad, Bernardino Licos, was from Busaoit, Bacnotan, La Union. Mom was born Flaviana Subido and grew up in Dangdangla, San Juan, La Union. They owned a lot of farm land that included valleys as well as mountainous and hilly countryside. The land supported crops like rice, sugar cane, tobacco, as well as other foods.

My parents also raised horses, chickens, carabaos (water buffalo), and goats. Tenant workers lived nearby. When my parents moved to another town, some of the tenants remained on our farm. I have strong memories of the planting and harvesting seasons. Dad told us never to go out to the farms as small children because we might get hurt. My sense of adventure led me to sneak out to the rice fields time after time just to get experience as a farmer.

Rufino at age 12, receiving
sixth grade diploma

I enjoyed farm life, especially during the rainy seasons. I swam in the fields when they were filled with rain water, and I swam in the brooks near our house. Dad insisted that we boys not become farmers. He wanted each of his sons to be well

20

educated and become a professional in some respectable business.

During my year in third grade, I became an altar boy at Saint Gabriel Catholic Church. That was a turning point in my life. When I graduated from sixth grade, I decided to enter the seminary and study for the priesthood. Mom was very religious; president of the Apostoladas, a religious organization for women, until she passed away. She favored my decision, but Dad, who was a catholic convert, would not give his permission for me to enter the seminary. I gave him one year to reconsider.

After my first year in high school in Bacnotan, I forced myself to enter the seminary, about three hundred miles away from home, regardless of Dad's refusal to approve my decision. In the eight years I studied at the seminary, Dad never came to visit me.

My seminary friends and I spent almost every summer vacation in Baguio City. We particular enjoyed stopping by our house where Dad and Mom prepared lunch for the entire group of about fifty students.

Young Rufino with friend at home in the Philippines

Life in the seminary was challenging under the German missionaries and Filipino priests. I developed my strong religious and character traits at that point of my life, and I can say with all my heart that it was the best thing that happened to me in my young life. I also developed my athletic skills in basketball, volleyball, tennis, soccer, swimming, and track.

When I was somewhere between fourteen and sixteen years old, I developed rheumatic enlargement of my heart. I was granted a sabbatical leave until I recovered. During that period, I weighed only seventy-two pounds.

Following my seminary days, I entered Saint Louis University of Baguio City. Two-and-a-half years later, I was told that I could graduate and immediately begin to teach at the university. However, I believed God had a better plan for me, and I devoted the next two years to teaching at the Antamok Tram mines. Then I moved to the city and taught at Maryhurst Minor Seminary in the morning and St. Louis University in the afternoon until I emigrated to the United States in 1968.

* * * * *

The loud burping of the telephone on my night stand wakened me. It took two or three seconds before I realized I was in Tokyo and on my way to the United States.

"Sir, it's your time to get up. Please be in the lobby in an hour," a pleasant female voice chirped in my ear.

I jumped out of bed and walked into the bathroom to brush my teeth and shower. In thirty minutes I was in the lobby. I waited for the rest of the group, making several guesses as to what the day held for me.

"Ladies and gentlemen, we are boarding the bus to bring us to the airport," a Japanese lady with a pleasant smile said. "I hope you had a good sleep. You will be served with breakfast in the plane. Please follow me."

I selected a window seat on the bus and enjoyed the view of the city with all its skyscrapers on the twenty-five minute drive to the airport. When we arrived at the airport, we checked in and waited for our flight. I realized I was feeling lightheaded from not sleeping and I took the opportunity of the short wait to doze.

At 8:00 a.m., we boarded a 747 Boeing JAL jet. As we taxied down the runway, the stewardess told us about our flight from Tokyo to Hawaii. She then advised us to fasten our seatbelts, adding that we would be served breakfast after we took off and reached cruising altitude and speed.

Once again I prayed for a safe trip. The plane lifted into the air and my heart started to beat stronger again. I closed my eyes and raised my head to counteract the pull of gravity.

"Coffee, orange juice, or tea?" the stewardess asked, startling me out of my thoughts. She handed me a tray and I ate my breakfast slowly, enjoying the food, coffee, and orange juice. At the same time, however, I pondered what should do when I arrived at Los Angeles Airport? I would not be met by friends or relatives because I had told no one in the United States of my trip. Nor had I signed a teaching contract with an American school, as had many emigrating teachers.

Uncle Castor, who had lived in Pasadena, California, near the Los Angeles Airport, had died in 1959. I looked at my watch, which was given to me, through my dad, by Uncle Caledonio (Uncle Castor's younger brother) when Uncle Celedonio visited the Philippines. Both Castor and Caledonio left the Philippines in 1926. How they came to America is not known.

"Are you finished with your breakfast?" the stewardess asked as she prepared to remove my tray.

I handed her the tray and fixed the table hinged to the seat in front of me. My mind continued to consider my problem of contacting my relatives when I reached Los Angeles. I occupied myself by standing and stretching, walking to the bathroom, wondering how other passengers could sleep so peacefully, while others with headphones listened to music so calmly.

July 22, 1968

CERTIFICATE OF CROSSING THE INTERNATIONAL DATE LINE

日付変更線通過記念証

Rufino A. Licos

This certificate officially proclaims that the bearer has crossed the International Date Line aboard a Jet Courier of Japan Air Lines.

松尾静磨

Shizuma Matsuo, President

JAPAN AIR LINES

Certificate presented to Rufino by Japan Air Lines when the plane in which he was flying crossed the International Date Line on its way to the United States on July 22, 1968.

Surely, my mind could not have been the only one with so many unanswerable questions racing through it. I smiled at those passengers who, like me, were anticipating their arrival in California. They all probably were being met by brothers, sisters, or relatives. How lucky they will be to be reunited with relatives they may not have seen for many years.

I looked through a window and admired the clouds under the plane. Mom, Dad, my brothers, and the many friends who came to see me off on my journey would be on their way back to the province where I was born.

As I gave her a farewell hug, I remember Mother telling me, "Son, be careful; don't trust strangers." Her eyes held tears of both sorrow for her and joy for me on that day.

"If we should never see each other again," she whispered to me through her tears, "remember that I always will be watching you and praying for you."

My thoughts turned to the events only weeks ago when I announced my decision to leave home.

Cousin Juana Aquino Almojera's wedding photograph with husband Norberto in Taboc, San Juan La Union.

Artemio had been puzzled when I said to him "Tell Mom and Dad to prepare for a party next weekend. Tell them that on June 30, 1968 – next Saturday – they are to invite all the teachers, relatives, and friends in town to our home for an important announcement."

The week passed quickly. I took the Dang-wa bus from Baguio to San Gabriel. I was a stranger to the other passengers. One older lady couldn't restrain her curiosity.

"Young man, where are you from?"

I smiled. "I teach at St. Louis University in Baguio. I'm just visiting my folks for the weekend."

"And who are your parents?"

"My parents own the rice mill and the grocery in town."

"Oh," she said, "Bernadino and Flaviana."

"Yes."

"They are very nice people."

I left the bus in front of our house. Mother was in the store and she came out to meet me.

"What is this? Why are you here? What are you doing to us? Your birthday is not until next month."

* * * * *

"Ladies and gentlemen, this is your stewardess. We are now crossing the International Date Line. Ahead of us it is the end of today; behind us is the beginning of tomorrow."

Everyone looked outside as they tried to digest that bit of information. Everyone was fascinated by the changing of today and tomorrow. It goes back to the time of creation when God created the world.

Stopover Hawaii

Ladies and gentlemen, the flight attendant said, "in a few hours we will be landing at the airport in Hawaii. If you have any items to declare at Customs, raise your hand and I will give you a Customs sheet on which you must write your name and everything valuable you are bringing to the United States as well as the cost of each item. The items you list will be checked by a Customs official at the airport.

"As soon as the plane lands, please remain seated and we"ll let you know when to get out of the plane. Go directly to the baggage claim then to Customs for your luggage check. Have your passport and carry-on luggage available to be checked. After everything is checked, we will board the same plane."

I realized that I was very nervous and didn't know exactly what to do. I followed the crowd and watched what the others did. I held on tightly to my hand-carries and my film negative.

These items were most important. I didn't worry about claiming luggage because I had only one hand-carry. I felt so sorry to some of the passengers ahead of me. Customs officials opened every piece of luggage they had. Some contained fruits and foods and these were confiscated because they could have been carrying bugs or germs.

Going through Customs didn't take long. An official asked for my declaration sheet, my photo negative, and my passport. I didn't know at that time that as soon as I passed through Customs I would receive my Green Card declaring that I was in the United States legally.

I stood awhile at a window in the airport lobby watching people passing by. Hawaii was an enchanting island, not much different from the Philippines. Coconut trees stood tall all around. Tropical plants and flowering plants grew abundantly. Many Asian people walked back and forth.

My thoughts turned back to the days when I would travel to Taboc, San Juan, La Union to visit my relatives, swim in the sea, and picnic under the coconut trees. The wonderful smell of fresh roasted fish, fresh boiled shellfish, and young coconuts seemed to fill my head. Those were days I never will forget.

Some passengers on the same plane were sitting on a bench and I joined them. Some were admiring the beauty of Hawaii. Others were making small talk about the trip and their plans when they reached California.

I started a conversation with a couple from Vigan, Ilocos Sur that also was traveling to America for the first time. Their son, who worked in San Francisco, had petitioned the government to grant the family visas. We enjoyed our conversation the more so because I had lived in their area during my high school and college days and I recognized some family names.

What time would we board again, I asked eventually. One lady looked kindly at me, smiled, and told me we would hear an announcement when the Customs check was completed and the plane was refueled for the last leg of our trip. No sooner had she spoken than an announcement came through the loudspeaker.

Destination California

L adies and gentlemen, Flight 210 JAL to San Francisco, is now boarding at Gate 4. The intercom announcer spoke with authority.

I picked up my carry-on luggage and lined up with the other passengers. Within minutes, I was in the same seat as before. I glanced for a final time at the Hawaii paradise island as the engine revved up. Then I closed my eyes and prayed. My heart began to beat faster again. My mind wandering far and near. I opened my eyes and looked around. Was I the only nervous person on board? Ah, forget about it. I'll be twenty-eight years old soon; old enough to handle this trip. If that's true, why am I suddenly beginning to perspire and felt uneasy?.

*   *   *   *   *

"Rufino, what's this party all about really?" Mom looked at me with great curiosity.

"We invited all your relatives and friends, and all the teachers. We asked Father Aspiras if you talked to him. He told us he was not informed about this party."

"Do you suspect that I might have arranged for a surprise wedding ceremony, Mom? Would you expect me to do something like that to you?"

Dad was unusually quiet that evening at supper. He stole an occasional glance at me out of the corner of his right eye.

"People will be arriving at twelve noon tomorrow," he offered. I did not reply.

The sun was bright on Saturday morning. I had slept late and I heard voices outside. Peering through my window, I saw relatives and friends cooking and chatting, or setting up tables and chair. I dressed quickly, went downstairs, ate a quick breakfast, and went outside to talk with my dad, who was directing the helpers. Florendo was talking to the cookers.

"So what's the good news?" Florendo asked me.

I looked at him and then at Dad, and smiled at them both without replying. Guests began to arrive.

"Happy birthday and thanks for the invitation," they greeted me. Lots of gifts were on the kitchen table. Mom looked at me but never said a word. I noticed that she was tense, as though suspecting unpleasant news.

A canopy and tables for the guests had been placed between the rice mill and the house. Some guests were drinking *basi*, a sugar cane wine. Others were enjoying beer or soda pop. More and more people gathered. Father Aspiras, our parish priest, arrived with some of the teachers. Guests flowed outside and inside. Some guests already sat on the table, chatting and laughing. Children played on both sides of the hedge. My oldest brother, Artemio, and his wife, Leonida arrived with their children. Florendo and his wife, Jovita, welcomed the guests as they came into the yard.

Archdiocesan Minor Seminary bishops, priests, and students in 1956-1957. Rufino is second from the left, row four.

"Father, will you please lead the prayer," Dad requested. Mom was standing beside me looking grim with apprehension as the guests quieted for the blessing. After Father Aspiras prayed over the food, the guests resumed their conversations and the noise level shot up again. Everyone was having a great time. The aroma of the food filled the air. In the midst of the festivities, a car arrived carrying my compadres from Baguio City, Mr. & Mrs Eliseo Malicdem and Mr.& Mrs. Romeo Sedano. It surely was a big celebration.

Dad waved both hands above his head. The loud laughter and conversation of the party guests slowly stopped. Dad looked around to get the full attention of our guests.

"Ladies and gentlemen and friends. This has been the most hectic week we have experienced in our lives. Our youngest son, Rufino, will explain the reason for this celebration."

He spoke in a clear but sad tone. Both Dad and Mom were in tears, sensing that something was about to happen that would severely affect their lives. It was only when I became the father of our wonderful daughters that I understood their feelings, the anticipation of an event that would change the structure of our lives forever.

Our guests noticed the tenseness of my parents and their former gaiety turned to somber expectation as their heads turned toward me. I stood slowly, looked at my friends, and said: "Please, wait for me while I get something upstairs."

I returned after ten minutes. Everyone was still quiet, consumed with curiosity.

"I'm really sorry to keep you waiting and wondering what's going on here. I'm holding in my left hand a huge envelope and in my right hand a smaller envelope. The larger envelope contains an X-ray negative attesting to the fact that I do not have tuberculosis or any similar disease. In my right hand is an envelope that holds my passport and an airplane ticket."

The silence was absolute. Not one person moved. I looked around the yard, swallowed hard, and continued.

"In three weeks I'll be leaving the Philippines to make a fresh start in the United States of America. I'll miss every one of you and I hope you will miss me."

Tears suddenly rolled down my cheeks as I tried to continue with my speech, but sounds came only in broken phrase,

"May I request that my brothers and sisters-in-law please take good care of our parents while I'm away. To all my relatives and friends, continue to visit and watch over my folks. I love you and I'll miss each of you until the day I return."

I sat down heavily on my chair. At first, there was no sound. Everyone seemed to be digesting the news. A Licos family member was about to leave the homeland. This had not been done in many years. What would become of him? Would he ever return? Would he be heard of again?

Rufino and Eppie with former nanny Dolor Licos during visit in 2002.

The same thoughts ran through my head. What indeed would happen to me now? My thoughts were interrupted by an outburst of talking and laughing as our friends absorbed my remarks and began to discuss the huge step that young Rufino was taking.

I suddenly realized that Mom and Dad were standing in front of me. Both were trying to act brave and nonchalant, but it wasn't working very well.

We all hugged and cried together. Then we felt better and began to discuss the momentous trip.

* * * * *

I put my hand-carry luggage in the compartment above my head. The airplane was parked next to the ocean and I was able to look through the window to watch wave after wave break on the shore. Men and women were sunbathing. Children were waddling in the water and on the beach. Farther from the shore, surfers and water gliders dotted the water and sky. Along the shoreline, waving leaves revealed dozens of coconuts high in the air almost ready for picking.

Maybe I should have made plans to live in Hawaii. I felt a small lump in my throat as I realized I could not return to the Philippines. Not yet. Not until I proved my value to myself and my family in America.

Lights flashed on and off ahead of me. Fasten seat belts. I heard click after click as the passengers around me obeyed the command. My own seat belt clicked obediently. An attendant gave instructions on the use of security equipment near me. The passengers were quiet as the plane began to move. I closed my eyes and leaned my head against the back of my seat. My right hand sought the security of the rosary my mother presented to me before I left the house, her hands closing around mine with a warmth and slight trembling that I would carry with me forever. I began to pray.

The take-off was smooth. As a veteran flier now, I was satisfied with the pilot's performance. Soon an attendant announced that we could unfasten our seat belts. Breakfast was served – again. This time we enjoyed a roll, coffee, milk or juice, and a small cup of fruit. I was so hungry that I devoured my food and drink in a few minutes.

I continued praying my rosary, thanking God for watching over me as I entered the United States of America. I could hardly believe I was in the United States. I felt great relief that my journey was going so smoothly.

The flashing signal reminded us to remain seated, fasten our seat belts, and extinguish cigarettes. I glanced at my watch and made some quick calculations. It would be 11:30 a.m. in San Francisco. I could see the Golden Gate bridge beneath my window. What a marvelous sight! It was breathtaking, sparkling in the brilliant sunlight. One of the greatest wonders of the world. How could people build this bridge by the ocean across so much water? It was very fascinating sight.

Suddenly, I felt the unexpected noise beneath the plane as the wheels swung down from the plane's belly. Swiftly we glided over the runway and I felt the tires touch the land. A wave of great relief overcame me. I felt cold air streaming from the overhead vents with the same force as a rapidly deflating balloon. Cold air from America. I was home, safe on the ground in my new home.

The plane made a right turn and there, beyond my window I saw the largest airport I could ever imagine. Planes were lined up according to their brand. Large and small trucks raced across tarmacs bent on errands that were unknown to me. People scurried near the buildings like ants racing for cover from the fierce noise of the engines. A man holding two long flashlights with red cones signaled to the pilot, guiding our plane into its landing position. Everyone seemed to know his or her exact task at this monstrous site. Everyone except me.

Passengers stopping in San Francisco began to remove their luggage from the overhead cabinets. Babies began to cry as the air pressure change stung their ears. I remained seated and quiet, watching with a certain amount of envy the faces of passengers who were alighting to meet family and friends. They had reached their dreamland and were anticipating a reunion just beyond the gate. I also had reached my dreamland, but I had no idea what lay beyond the gate.

Soon we left San Francisco and it's wonderful bridge behind us as we traveled south to our next destination. This is where I would alight to make my fortune in my new home. I felt like a track runner waiting at the starting line. Up until now, I had only to dream about the race ahead. Now the starter's whistle was about to sound and I must be ready to spring ahead onto my chosen track of life.

"Ladies and gentlemen, welcome to Los Angeles, California We will land in about fifteen minutes. After the engines stop and the door opens, please take all your belongings with you and proceed to the luggage claim. We hope you enjoyed your flight with us and that we see you again."

The *no smoking* and *fasten your seatbelt* signs came on again. I peered out the window and was amazed at the immense size of Los Angeles sprawled beneath me. I closed my eyes and thanked God that we landed safely. When the plane came to a complete stop, I stood up and stretched my legs.

The main door opened. Many passengers already had gathered their belongings and were moving slowly toward the door. I waited for everyone from the back rows to leave before I took my initial step. As I passed an attendant who was standing by the door, she said to me, "Goodbye, sir, and good luck."

"Thank you," I answered with a smile, " I may need a good amount of luck."

Finding Uncle Celedonio

My first sight of America as my feet touched the ground in the continental USA was a group of young men and women wearing the same outfit as those in the plane. Am I in America or somewhere else, I asked myself. The young men and women were very friendly. They smiled and bowed to me as I passed them. I learned later that they called themselves Hippies and they were promoting a more relaxed lifestyle.

The airport was bustling with airline personnel, families going on vacation, business men and women, police officers, and many people who were just sitting and watching the moving scenery. I could do that, so I also sat. In fact, at the moment, that's about all I could do since I had no other plan.

My attention was drawn to the variety of different nationalities and spoken languages in the area where I was sitting. Some people were checking in, purchasing tickets, walking back, and forth and constantly looking at their watches. In one corner, two affectionate girls were doing their own thing. When I glanced at them second time, they were facing me and I realized that one of the "girls" was a guy with very long hair.

A child about four years old looked at me and smiled. I returned the smile. He seemed to be very friendly kid. Suddenly, I noticed he was sitting beside me as though I was his father. Eventually, his parents came along from somewhere and collected him. He waved at me as he left.

Whenever I stood up, I carried my hand-carry luggage with me. I went closer to the telephone booth and observed how people started the phone by dropping coins into the top of the black box before they dialed. In the Philippines, we simply gave a dime to the sales clerk before we used the phone.

I returned to my seat and consulted my watch and the watch on the wall. Indeed, there was a great difference in time between Los Angeles and the Philippines. It was fourteen hours ahead in Baguio.

Two and one-half hours had passed since I arrived at Los Angeles and I was no closer to making my next move. The weird thought occurred to me that I might make history by being the first person to live out his life in the Los Angeles Airport.

A kind-looking lady approached me and asked what flight I was waiting for and where was I going. I replied that I was not flying anywhere, just resting. She smiled and wished me well before continuing on her way. I should have asked her where she was going and confessed that I desperately needed help.

My mind was racing, considering solutions to the immediate problem of how to find my uncle who lived in America. Another uncle who emigrated to America had died in 1959. We had not called or written to Uncle Celedonio and he would not have suspected that a nephew would be knocking on his door without warning. How might I locate him in this huge country? How should I introduce myself?

I walked toward the phone booth and quietly stood behind an older man who was speaking into the telephone. He was telling someone the time he would be arriving at his destination in Milwaukee, Wisconsin, and asking his wife to meet him at the airport. As he continued to talk, he noticed my presence.

"Would you like to use the phone, young man?"

I fingered the crisp one hundred dollar bill in my wallet, my only money.

"Yes, sir, I do, but I don't know the phone number of my uncle," I answered. I must have looked sad; the man beckoned me to wait, quickly finished his conversation over the telephone, turned to me, and sized up my probable condition.

"Did you just arrive in the country?" he asked.

"Yes, sir, from the Philippines."

"Welcome to America." He smiled broadly and put out his hand. I shifted my bag to my left hand and took his firm grip.

We introduced ourselves by name and he continued, "Where does your uncle live, Rufino?"

"He lives in a city called Santa Maria, near Arroyo Grande, sir, but I don't know in which state that is."

"You're in great luck, Santa Maria is in California where you are now. The city is only about two hundred miles north of us. Do you have his telephone number?"

"No, Sir, I have no information except his name."

"And what is your uncle's name?"

"Celedonio Licoscos, sir."

I decided not to trouble the kind gentleman with the knowledge that while most of the family had shortened our last name to Licos, Uncle Celedonio had kept our original name.

"Do you have money to call him on the telephone?"

My right hand went to my pocket and brought out the single bill that I possessed.

"I have one hundred dollars," I said, "but I don't know how to get the right amount of change to make a telephone call."

The man smiled and waved for me to put the bill back in my pocket. He then turned to the telephone, put in a coin and conversed with someone at the other end.

"Yes, operator, I would like the telephone number of Celedonio Licoscos, in Santa Maria, please."

A moment later, he turned and asked: "Do you want to talk with Celedonio Licoscos Junior or Senior?"

"He lives in Santa Maria, sir," I stumbled.

"Yes, but two men by that name live in Santa Maria. One is called Senior and the other is called Junior. Which is your uncle?"

"Probably the senior, sir."

The man took a pen from his shirt pocket and wrote a telephone number on a piece of paper that also came from his shirt pocket. He thanked the operator and hung up the phone. A dime dropped from the phone and he put it back into the proper slot on top of the box. Once again he engaged an operator in conversation, giving her my name. Then he handed the telephone to me and stepped back.

I took the receiver and was about to speak when I heard a female voice say: "I have a collect call for Celedonio Licoscos Senior from Rufino Licos. Will you accept the charges?"

"From Rufino Licos? In the Philippines? What's he calling me for?" a deep and gruff voice came through the telephone line.

34

"Sir, will you accept the charges?" the operator cut in.

"Not from the Philippines," he replied in disbelief.

"Uncle Celedonio," cried in terror. I was about to lose my contact with one of my only relatives in America. I didn't know what it meant to accept the charges, but I imagined that if he refused, our conversation would come to a quick close..

"I'm Rufino, the son of your brother, Bernardino," I pleaded.

"One moment, please," the operator cut in again. "Sir, will you accept the charges?"

"Where is this call coming from?" my uncle asked gruffly.

"From Los Angeles, sir. Will you accept the charges?"

"Oh, all right," my uncle answered in a resigned tone.

"Thank you, sir. Go right ahead with your call, sir."

There was a pause. Neither of us knew what to say at the moment. Finally, Uncle Celedonio spoke.

"So you're Bernardino's boy? Where are you?"

His voice didn't sound too friendly, but I realized that my uncle was startled to hear from any member of the family.

"I am at the Los Angeles Airport, Uncle," I answered.

"Why are you here?"

"I've come to live in America!"

"Oh. When did you arrive?"

"About three hours ago, Uncle."

"And you just called now? Why didn't you let me know you were coming? Didn't your dad tell you what to do when you got here? How far is Santa Maria from Los Angeles?"

Celedonio's voice got louder by the sentence. Without giving me time to reply to his questions, he lectured me for almost twenty minutes, mostly at the top of his lungs. I gave up trying to talk. I was just so happy to have contacted a relative. Eventually, he stopped yelling and told me to go to find out the time of the next flight to Santa Maria.

I turned around and found the kind gentleman who had arranged the call still behind me. I explained my immediate mission and he held the telephone for me while I ran to the information desk.

"Excuse me, madame, is there a flight to Santa Maria yet,?" I asked one of the ladies at an information desk counter.

"It left just five minutes ago."

I returned to the telephone and reported to my uncle. After a pause, he instructed me to return to the desk and find out if there was a bus going to Santa Maria. Again, I handed the telephone to my benefactor and ran to the desk.

"There are Greyhounds around the corner," I was told. "Find one that has a card on it saying *Santa Maria*." I cocked my head and wondered how greyhound dogs could carry people long distances.

"I was looking for a bus, not a dog," I said in confusion.

The lady laughed and explained that the bus company was called Greyhound.

"You won't be riding on a dog, I can assure you," she said gently, the smile remaining on her face.

I raced back to the telephone and told my uncle that I would get on the next Greyhound and meet him in Santa Maria. He said that was fine and he hung up without asking how he would identify me. As I thought about it, there probably wouldn't be too many young Filipinos arriving on the bus, and if I tried to appear lost – which wouldn't be hard to do under the circumstances – he would pick me out from the crowd. Uncle Celedonio sounded like a man who was easily annoyed by details and inconveniences.

I placed the receiver on the hook and turned to the wonderful American who had helped me so much during my first hours in the continental United States. As I thanked him for his courtesy and patience, he handed me a five dollar bill. The one hundred dollar bill in my pocket wouldn't be very helpful, he said, because it would be hard to exchange for smaller bills.

Again, I thanked him and asked him to write his name and address for me on a slip of paper so I could repay him. He did so, wished me success in America, and walked out of my life – until much later.

As I stood in the Los Angeles airport, little did I realize that my next trip through the buildings would be as an award-winning educator with a wife and three of our four daughters on a trip from Wisconsin to Disneyland.

The Sun

As I walk back along my long traveled years
  Recalls the bitter and sweet memories;
Young to things yet unknown and unseen
  Presents the new life again on the screen.

Now grown and full grown to suck knowledge
  Opens to novels of skin and edge;
So soothe but grief and love for all
  Born to care whoever seems to fall.

Life peeps like the sun on cloudy noon
  Reminds that life darkens anon;
Yet brightens on the face of the earth
  Proves that death is a rebirth.

7-30-68

Chapter 2: Getting Started

As I reached the corner of the airport, a bus bearing the placard *Santa Maria* stopped in front of me. I climbed aboard and handed the driver my five dollar bill. In return, I received a one dollar bill that I carefully put into my pocket next to the one hundred dollar bill. There were ten people on the bus. I took the seat directly behind the driver and turned around to see the other passengers, hoping to identify a typical American.

An older lady was sleeping. A man in front of her was reading a book. A young woman and young man on the other side of the aisle were dressed in unusual clothes and were hugging each other. Another man sitting two seats behind me kept on smiling in a way that was scary. I thought he might be crazy. I decided that the passengers on this bus did not represent typical Americans.

As the bus prepared to pull away from the airport, I stood up by my seat and took stock of my situation. I had crossed the Pacific Ocean successfully, I had made contact with my uncle only a few hours from the Los Angeles Airport, and all the Americans I had met so far were friendly and helpful. What was to happen next?

It was 5:45 in the afternoon when the bus driver twisted around and said to me, "you'll have to change to another bus at Ventura because this bus does not go to Santa Maria. I'll let you know when we reach there."

He seemed to be a very nice and helpful middle-aged man. I didn't know what to do: sleep or read. I sat down and let my mind wander. Five more passengers entered the bus before the driver shut the door. The bus began to move. I leaned back in my seat. "Come what may," I whispered.

I looked out through the glass window onto the lifestyle of Los Angeles. The sidewalks were crowded with busy people going in every direction, people of different nationalities, people of different color, people intent on being successful in whatever they chose to do. The sun was still bright. Men and women on the streets shaded their eyes from the bright sun as they talked and laughed. I repeated a single phrase over and over as if to assure myself that I had made the right decision to leave my family and strike out on my own: "This is America!"

As the bus rolled northward along Highway 101, I expected to see many of the tall buildings that I had read about and seen in movies and books. America was filled with tall buildings, tall people with tall desires, and tall dreams coming true. Where were the tall buildings? We passed only low, one- and two-level houses and stores. Where were the buildings and people I had seen in the movies?

Our first stop was in the city of Oxnard, sixty miles northwest of Los Angeles. Some passengers left the bus and others climbed aboard. The driver got out for about ten minutes and then returned and started up the bus again. We traveled another eight miles and came to Ventura where I changed to another bus.

We could see the Pacific Ocean on our left for almost thirty miles as we drove toward Santa Barbara. The sight of the great ocean made me homesick. Thousands of miles across the water, my family probably was worrying about me. Had I arrived safely in America? Did I find a relative? Was I safe?

As soon as I boarded the next bus that would take me to Uncle Celedonio, I remained in my seat with my eyes shut and my head pressed gently against the back of the seat. I must have dozed off for an hour; I wakened when the bus came to a halt.

"We are now in Santa Maria," the driver declared. "Please take all your luggage with you."

I was the last to leave the bus. My watch confirmed that it was fifteen minutes after midnight. In the waiting room, I took a seat in a corner and held tightly to my luggage. Who will pick me up, I wondered?

The Greyhound Bus station certainly wasn't crowded. Three of us sat apart from each other, each concerned with our own little world of personal activities.

I picked up a magazine that was on the table and tried to read. Who was going to meet me? How would he or she recognize me? How would this next journey in my new life begin?

As time passed, I began to wonder if anyone was going to meet me. Then a beautiful, young lady with brunette hair came into the room. She was wearing a blue dress, a pair of white earrings, and white low-heeled shoes. She stood at the door for a moment and then came directly to where I was sitting.

"Are you my cousin, Rufino?"

I looked intently at her but didn't answer right away. She was beautiful, an adorable young lady, certainly not of Filipino extraction. I didn't know what to do. Stand up? Embrace her?

"Excuse me, who are you?"

"Oh I'm sorry. My name is Andrée. I'm your cousin's wife. My father-in-law, Celedonio, is at work right now and he asked me to pick you up."

I stood up and reached for Andrée's hand to shake it. Instead, she put both arms around me and hugged me.

"Welcome to the United States, Cousin," she said brightly.

Releasing her hold on me, she picked up my small piece of luggage and instructed me to follow her. As she walked ahead of me, she turned back and asked:

"How was your trip?"

"Tiresome."

"Were there a lot of people in the bus?"

"When we started at the airport about a third of the bus was occupied, but we picked up more passengers along the way. We had only five left when we reached here."

I didn't move my eyes away from Andrée during our drive. I was still enchanted by her beauty. She truly was an angel.

"Here we are, Cousin. This is our home."

It was a ranch-type house. She took out my luggage from the trunk and invited me in inside.

"This is your room, Cousin The bathroom is on the right."

Andrée handed me a towel.

"Wash up and then come to the kitchen. I prepared something for you to eat. I imagine that you must be tired and starving. After you eat, you can get some rest. My husband, Cel Junior, will be home from work at 7:30 in the morning."

After washing up, I went to the kitchen. Andrée had prepared fried rice, barbecued beef, salad, and a glass of milk. A glass of milk? I never liked milk. I drank milk when I was in grade school and I always had diarrhea. From that time on, I never drank milk. I sat down, thank her and asked for a glass of water instead.

Andrée sat across me and I enjoyed the food she prepared. We had a nice chat about my long trip. We laughed so hard when I told her about some of my hilarious and unforgettable experiences between the Philippines and Santa Maria.

When I went to my room, I couldn't sleep. I turned on the television and glanced at the clock on the bureau. It was 3:20 a.m. I must have dozed off when I heard knocking at the door.

"Hi, cousin Rufino. How are you?"

The younger Celedonio came in and gave a hug.

"I hope you were able to sleep. I just got back from work", he continued.

I followed him to the kitchen and joined him for a cup of coffee. We talked for a long time about our lives, my ambitions, and his work.

I told him to go and rest but he insisted that he come with us to Uncle Celedonio's home. My uncle and auntie were still in bed when we got to their house. We entered at the rear door since Uncle Cel's house was under construction. The entire house was almost completely torn down. We came into the kitchen. The sink was filled with dirty dishes, cups, glasses, and utensils. Pots and pans were on top of the stove. Four loaves of bread, three bottles of jelly, and a sack of potatoes were on the table. Andrée looked at me and smiled. My cousin, Cel Jr, went to wake up Uncle and Auntie.

"So, this is my nephew, Rufino? Welcome to the states," Uncle Celedonio said, giving me a big hug. I soon felt a lot more comfortable talking to him now than when I had called from the airport. He was much like my own dad. He looked a little bit younger than Dad, but seemed to be less energetic.

Cousin Cel Junior and Andrée said goodbye after a few minutes. I thanked them for their hospitality and for bringing me to Uncle Celedonio's house. Uncle Cel then asked me about our families in the Philippines. He dozed off occasionally. Aunt Mabel explained that he had worked all night at a restaurant. She continued to chat, telling me stories about their life. Uncle Cel wakened to join in our conversation now and then. At other times, he snored so loudly that I could not help but smile.

"Cel usually sleeps on that couch for hours and hours when he comes home from work," Aunt Mabel commented. "Sometimes, he forgets to eat lunch and I let him sleep until he's fully rested. As soon as I wake up, I eat my breakfast and then I go out to feed the chickens and pigs that we keep behind the house. We have three acres of land here and this has been my life since the boys grew up and left home."

I learned that Uncle Cel was in the U.S. Navy. He and Aunt Mabel have three boys: Celedonio Jr., Paul, and James. She told me that they all live very close to them and that I would have an opportunity to meet each of them.

As I got to know my uncle better, I was struck by how, although he had been in America for a long time, he continued to retain all the Filipino characteristics, ways, family values, thought processes, and respect for both young and old. His home life was important to him. He was a hard-working father, very religious, caring, and patient. He used every corner of his land – another Filipino characteristic.

We talked for hours about all different walks of life. Aunt Mabel sat in her own particular seat and place at the right hand side of my uncle. I, too, sat to the left of my uncle, across from my aunt. We spent most of our breakfast, lunch and dinner at a table close to the kitchen. Nearby was a formal cherry table and twelve hand-carved matching chairs. The impressive dining set seemed to have been designed for a royal family.

Against the wall on the right side was a wooden, intricately designed china cabinet. On its shelves was the most beautiful set of antique plates and matching cups and glasses that I had ever beheld. If a visitor were to examine only these pieces, they surely would conclude that the Licoscos were a wealthy couple.

The kitchen itself seemed topsy turvy due to the construction of the house. They were remodeling their one-level home. The living room as of that time was good enough for the two of them being untouched by the construction project. They had beautiful, expensive couches and chairs. The couches were covered with comfortable linen for me to sleep on at night. A large, wide-screen television in one corner of the living room provided me with nightly entertainment. Johnny Carson's late night talk show ended each day before I sent to sleep.

Uncle Cel shifted in his comfortable chair, trying hard to remain awake. I could tell by the heaviness of his eyelids that he really wanted to sleep. My arrival had been totally unexpected and Uncle Cel had recently completed a thirteen-hour work shift that began the previous day at 5:00 p.m.

Aunt Mabel seemed to chew on some type of food during all her waking hours. A long-time diabetic, she found comfort in munching between meals each day.

Uncle Cel mastered his body's crying out for sleep, and we continued to talk for hours about the family and the Philippines. I could tell that he was homesick and would like to visit his homeland. I also knew that Mabel would not allow him to do so. She had returned to the Islands with him in 1960 and let it be known that she was not impressed with the Filipino way of life. There would be no more trips across the ocean for her and, if she had her way, there would be no more trips for Uncle Celedonio.

Aunt Mabel sat comfortably on her chair to the right of Cel. I sat on his left side across from Mabel. I learned as the days went by that we always sat around a table in the small kitchen.

The master bedroom was wide enough to be converted into two bedrooms if need be. They slept on a huge oak, king-size bed that was topped by an overhead canopy decorated with beautiful blue and white flowers. My initial impression was that my uncle and auntie lived most comfortably.

During my first week in America, I was driven around Grover City, a small community one hundred and eighty miles north of Los Angeles. Almost immediately, one of my long-standing beliefs was shattered.

I had grown up with the understanding that white Americans were not farmers; they either were cowboys or grand people living in huge buildings. Of course, I had heard about farmers, factory workers, apple pickers, sugar cane planters in Hawaii, maids, helpers, and other such workers, but I thought these people were only blacks, Asians, or poor immigrants who were seeking to improve their lives.

As we drove through the valley farmland, I saw white American farmers who lived in small one-level houses that had only two or three bedrooms. Then, with mounting nervousness, I sat quietly as Uncle Celedonio parked his white 1960 Lincoln Continental car by the side of the road. He stepped out onto the ribbon of pavement – there didn't seem to be any dirt roads in America – walked quickly to the adjacent field, and picked a head of lettuce. A few minutes later, he stopped again and selected a cabbage head.

"What are you doing, Uncle?" I asked in alarm.

"Getting some food for our dinner," he answered calmly as he drove on.

"But, you're stealing a farmer's produce," I said. "Won't the farmers get mad at you?"

"Not at all," he replied calmly. "They allow people to pick a few of their vegetables as long as we don't do it all the time. As it happens, I know most of these farmers. They're Filipino friends who farm this valley."

I digested this bit of information, but my initial curiosity remained about who actually worked American farms.

"Uncle, do white Americans really work on farms?"

Uncle Celedonio looked over at me and shook his head from side to side.

"You don't seem to know your American history," he said quietly. "America is a great country because people can do whatever they want to do. Tens of thousands of white Americans work on farms because they love farming. I work in a restaurant because I like to work in a restaurant. You're going to work at some trade because you want to do that kind of work, not because you have to do it."

Uncle Celedonio gave me a look that a schoolmaster might give a dull student. He had become a loyal American and was proud of the freedoms most Americans take for granted in this great land that is 3,000 miles from east to west and 2,300 miles from north to south.

Down the road, we stopped to see two friends who had emigrated from Balaoan, La Union in the Philippines. Gualberto was a retired older man who had married a much younger woman. This practice is far more common among Filipinos than it is among Americans. Many Filipino men come to America and work hard to succeed in their profession. At some point, they realize they need a companion in life.

At the same time, many young Filipino women dream of settling in the United States. An accepted practice is for the young ladies to marry older men who have carved out comfortable lives through years of hard work. Some women marry men who are older than their own fathers.

Conrado and Lara from La Union are happily married even though Conrado is thirty-two years older than Lara. Despite the great difference in ages, God blessed them with one son. Almost every weekend, Uncle Cel drove my auntie and me to Conrado and Lara's home to visit and, often, to enjoy lunch or supper. We talked for hours about life in the Philippines. They especially enjoyed listening to my stories because they both were homesick. Living where they did in California was like living in the Philippines because of the climate, people, and customs of the area.

Each morning I helped Uncle Cel prepare the foundation of his house. My task was to mix cement and pour the heavy slush between the wood framing of the floor. It was hard work, but during the two in a half months that I was with them, we finished the foundation, roof, and walls.

During my stay in California, I met Cousins Paul, James, and Cel Jr. We enjoyed weekend get-togethers as they took me around to meet more Filipinos.

I applied for my state teaching license within a few weeks of arriving in California. I passed the state examination for teaching with flying colors and interviewed to fill openings in mathematics, English and Spanish because I was well qualified in those areas.

Rufino with his California Liscoscos cousins. Front row: Rufino, James; rear: Paul, Celedonio Jr. – 1979.

Much to my regret, when the state officials learned that I had no working experience in America, I was not given the opportunity to teach in California.

Shortly after California became my temporary home, I learned of a talent competition to be held in Santa Maria. Uncle Cel suggested that I enter the contest if I had a talent. Many years before, I had learned to balance glasses and other objects on my head while dancing and performing acrobatics.

Rufino performs a water glass balancing act in Waterloo, Wisconsin in 1973.

I competed among many contestants who represented twenty-four nationalities with a glass-balancing acrobatic dance. Uncle Cel was surprised when I took first place. The following week, I was asked to drive up to San Francisco and audition to perform on television.

Teaching was my priority, however, and I continued to look in that direction, even though I continued to dance and balance objects around the country for many years.

45

Chapter 3: Richland Center

When I learned that teaching was not an option in California, I considered applying for a position in New York State. I also had heard good reports about teaching in Minnesota and I sent an application to that state in September 1968. Still, however, I remained interested in traveling to New York City, the best-known American city to those living in the Philippines. I wanted to see New York City for myself.

It was obvious that my educational background would play an important role in establishing myself in the United States. Because of my studies and teaching in the Philippines, I could be licensed to teach English, Spanish, Latin, mathematics, social science, and natural science in America.

While development of educational or trade skills in the Philippines remains an asset to those who are considering coming to America, it is not absolutely necessary. This country is filled with people who lead successful lives because they know how to do something well.

In 1968, the states of Idaho, Oregon, Washington, and Wisconsin were looking for math teachers. Math was one of my specialties and one that I thoroughly enjoyed teaching. I carefully studied the background of the four states and found myself particularly attracted to Wisconsin with its large acreage of dairy land and four distinct seasons of spring, summer, fall, and winter. I had not yet experienced snow, and that prospect also turned my search toward the northern part of the country.

I applied to the Wisconsin Department of Public of Instruction first. While I was waiting for a reply, I visited friends in the state of Minnesota, on the western border of Wisconsin.

As the guest of friends, I decided it would be helpful if I cleaned their apartment while they were at work. I began with the carpeted floors, getting on my hands and knees to pick up each little flake of dirt and dust. It was a long, long task.

When the couple returned home that evening, I told them what I had accomplished. After the laughter stopped, the husband went to a closet, pulled open the door, and introduced me to a vacuum cleaner, an appliance I had never seen. Carefully, and still chuckling, he showed me how to plug it in, start the motor, and clean the carpeting in minutes while standing up, rather than in hours on my hands and knees.

It took only a few days to receive an invitation to apply to Richland Center High School in central Wisconsin north of the state's capital city of Madison. I took a Greyhound bus almost immediately to meet with Gene Saucke, superintendent of the Richland Center School District.

The drive from Minnesota to Richland Center was exciting. The trip took almost eight hours and I slept part of the way, but I also spent many hours admiring the luscious scenic views, the splendid colors of the leaves, and the refreshing fall air.

It was about eight in the evening when I arrived at the Richland Center depot. Within ten minutes, a tall, good-looking man in his late 40s entered the waiting room. I knew that he must be Gene Saucke because he was wearing a suit and tie.

"Mr. Licos?" he said to me as he approached.

"Yes, sir. Good evening," I returned.

He looked at me carefully, smiled and asked:

"Are you really old enough to be a teacher? You look like a teenager, Mr. Licos."

Indeed I was a very young-looking man who weighed a modest ninety-eight pounds. We joked pleasantly about my appearance as Mr. Saucke drove me to the high school, six blocks from the bus depot. When we arrived, I met the school principal, James Schriver, a middle-aged man over six feet tall, well built, and very soft spoken.

"This is Mr. Licos," Mr. Saucke said, "I couldn't believe at first that he was old enough to be a teacher. He looked so young, short, and thin. I thought at first he was one of the students."

Mr. Schriver smiled and shook my hand. After we chatted for half an hour and got to know a bit about each other, he handed me the school's geometry and algebra text books.

"Mr. Licos, these are the text books we're using in the classroom. If you join our faculty, you will be our fourth math teacher since the school year began. We can't seem to find a math teacher who meets our needs."

That statement gave me not much assurance at all, but I tried not to show my concern. I already was convinced that Mr. Schriver was a good-natured and professional administrator who would be an understanding and an easy-going principal, even though he would demand the best performance of each teacher.

At last, Mr. Schriver stood and looked at me in a kindly manner. Holding out his hand again, he said:

"I supposed you must be tired from your trip. I"ll see you in my office tomorrow before school starts."

So saying, he left his office. Mr. Saucke drove me back to the Park Hotel, helped me register, and then arranged for me to remain at the hotel until I found an apartment – provided I joined the faculty.

We met again at 7:30 in the morning shortly after I enjoyed a cup of coffee and toast in the hotel restaurant. Mr. Saucke took me to Mr. Schriver's office and I was assigned to observe a geometry class being held in a portable classroom building outside the school.

Students began to arrive shortly after I entered the room. Everyone noticed me at the back of the room, but no one spoke to me. It wasn't that they appeared unfriendly; they were unsure of who I was, so they left well enough alone and didn't become involved for the moment.

For my part, I remained quiet and watchful. My curiosity was raised about the height of the students – they all were taller than my five foot three inches. They had fascinating colors in their hair, mostly sparkling blue eyes, and smooth skin.

Eventually, a girl turned around and gave me a dazzling smile. I responded with what I hoped was a dazzling smile of my own. It didn't frighten her so I guess my attempt was all right.

"Hi, I'm Amy. How are you?"

"Fine, thank you."

"What's your name? Where are you from? Are you the new foreign student?"

"My name is Rufino Licos from the Philippines. Yes, I guess you might call me a foreign student of a sort."

The students digested that brief dialog and went about their normal chatting until the teacher arrived. She was a tall, middle-aged, woman, who wore attractive glasses. The students continued to chatter as she took the roll call. She apparently knew most of the twenty-five teenagers well, calling them by their first name.

She started the lesson by going right to the blackboard and dividing it into two columns.– statements on the left side of the line and proofs on the right side. On top of each side she wrote the given parts of the problem and what needed to be proven.

One of the students turned to a companion and whispered:

"How did she get the answer?"

"I don't know," the other replied.

On another part of the board, the teacher wrote the second problem. Two students raised their hands.

"How did you get the answer that three sides of one triangle are congruent to the three sides of the second triangle?"

The teacher looked at me for the first time and smiled, as if to say "this is what I have to put up with."

"That's the given answer in the book," she answered.

The class then asked a lot of questions, many of which the teacher was unable to answer because math wasn't her field of study. I sat through the class period without saying a word.

Two more classes followed practically the same procedure. The fourth hour was my lunch period. I walked to the cafeteria and joined the line of the students. No one spoke to me as I got my food. Again, they weren't rude; they just were not sure how to strike up a conversation.

Mr. Schriver was standing by the cafeteria, supervising the students. When he saw me, he took my arm and led me to the lounge where I was introduced to a number of teachers who already were eating lunch. Some of them were curious about my presence and asked me many questions. Most of them became my close friends over the next months.

Back in the classroom, I observed Algebra 1 and modern math sessions. After school, Mr. Saucke picked me up while I was discussing my first day's experience with Mr. Schriver. Mr. Saucke and I had a great talk about my first day. He drove me to the hotel and remained for a cup of coffee in the restaurant. Before he left, he told me that I needed to buy some winter clothes, a winter coat, and boots since it was getting cold.

The Park Hotel a three-story, red brick building, was six blocks from the high school. Many traveling businessmen spent their evenings and weekends at the hotel because of its central location and it being the only hotel in Richland Center. College students coming from out of town to attend University of Wisconsin Extension classes also stayed there. I alternated eating breakfast and dinner at the hotel and one of the other restaurants in town.

My first weekend was spent mostly watching television in the hotel lobby and walking around the city. In the evening, many hotel guests watched TV and chatted with me. Talking to strangers was like talking to people you have known for a long time. Being new to Wisconsin, I learned a lot about people's lives, their business, travels, experiences, and even their family life. Sad to note, some guests were divorced and lonely men.

My natural curiosity prompted me to ask several people about the causes of divorces in this country since divorce was not acceptable in the Philippines at that time. I learned that most divorces in the United States are caused by incompatibility, cheating husbands or wives, financial difficulties, and poor family relationships.

College students who did not go home on weekends occasionally watched football games with me. I became so caught up with the drama in a good football game that I sometimes forgot to tend to my other responsibilities.

Simplifying Mathematics

On the Friday of my last day to observe classes before I began to teach, the substitute teacher attempted to explain a lesson in geometry. One of the students could not understand how the teacher came up with the answer to a problem. The teacher knew the answer because it was in her lesson plan, but she didn't know how the answer was obtained.

She looked toward me in the back of the room. Quickly, I waved my hand indicating that she should not turn to me because I did not want to let the students know who I was until Monday. But the hard-pressed teacher was at her wits end and she blurted out that I would know the answer.

"I'll ask Mr. Licos to explain the answer to your question," she said.

Of course, everyone looked at me. A student who sat at the back said:

"Are you a teacher? I thought you were an AFS student."

"Well, I am just observing your class."

"Mr. Licos will be your teacher starting Monday," the frustrated teacher continued.

Now I had everyone's attention. I stood up and approached the board.

"I'm in your class today only to observe and see if I can handle the subjects,"I explained. "However, since I was called by your teacher to explain the basis for a problem, I will do so.

"You must pay special attention because I have a very strong accent. English is one of the two official languages of the Philippines, but we all have a native accent in our words and phrases that is different from your accents and phrases. In America some people speak with a southern drawl, a Brooklyn accent, a New England accent, or an Ozark twang. Until I learn to speak like a Wisconsinite, you'll have to learn to understand a Filipino accent. Don't hesitate to ask me to repeat myself if you don't understand a word or sentence. I'll learn to speak better Wisconsinite if you help me."

I was pleased that they smiled and sat back in a relaxed fashion. I erased the board and started to read the problem.

"Understanding the problem is the basis for solving it. If you don't understand what's expected from you in the first reading, don't feel alone. That happens to me all the time. Just start again and read the words slowly. As soon as you think you're lost, begin again until each sentence makes sense. If you don't understand the question, you can't possibly be expected to determine the answer."

I wrote on the board the given parts of the problem we were studying. Then I wrote what was going to be proved in the problem. I divided the board into two vertical halves and wrote *Statements* on the left side and *Proofs* on the right side. I told them again to put down their pencils or pens and listen very attentively because of my strong accent. They did what I asked and remained very quiet.

"First of all, we're going to read the problem slowly and you're going to put up your hand as soon as you don't understand a word or idea."

I explained to them the part of the problem that was given, that is, that we had two triangles, and then we had what was to be proved, that is, that the triangles were congruent. The initial confusion in their minds was that they didn't know what *congruent* meant, so I told them that we simply were trying to show that one triangle would fit perfectly upon the other.

"Now we have a riddle to solve. This is a game. Look at the two triangles. Which parts of the triangles do we know are equal in length and connecting angles?"

We were given the lengths and angles of two sides of the triangle, they agreed.

"And what are we trying to prove?"

"That the two triangles were congruent by the use of the principle SSS ≅ SSS, where "S" stands for *side*. Thus, if three sides of one triangle are congruent – meaning equal – to three

51

sides of the second triangle, then the triangles are congruent. Now then, if two sides already are given, what's missing."

There was a bit of head scratching, but the students now were seeing the solution as a game and not a boring math problem, and they were having fun with finding the solution.

"We're just missing the third side," one student spoke up.

They worked that out quickly because they understood what they were trying to accomplish. After I wrote all the steps on the blackboard under the statements section, I asked the students if something was missing before we could prove the triangles were congruent.

"Not any more," one student called out and the class laughed and congratulated each other."

"Wow, that was simple," another student said, "once we knew what we were looking for."

I got up very early on Monday. I had not slept well because I was too excited and too nervous. I showered, dressed, and went down to the hotel restaurant.

"I'll have a cup of coffee, a small glass of orange juice, one egg, and two slices of toast, please."

A simple, uncomplicated order was called for this morning, I told myself. What could be more simple than the order I just gave to the waitress?

It turned out that I had no idea how many ways there were to prepare an egg. Boiled, or scrambled were the only ways we prepared eggs back in the Philippines. The patient waitress and I had a long conversation.

"How do you want your egg?"

"What are the possibilities, besides boiled or scrambled?"

"Fried, poached, or omelet."

"I recognize fried, though I've never had one. I'll have my egg fried, please."

"How do you want your fried egg cooked, Mr. Licos?"

"I'm well over my head now. Again, what are the possibilities for cooked fried eggs?"

"Well, you can have them sunny side up, over easy, or over hard. There are some variations of those choices, but let's just stay with the basics this morning, shall we?"

I could tell that the waitress was considering what deserted island I came from. But she continued to smile and hold her order pad ready, waiting for my response.

"What would you recommend for a man who has never had a fried egg?"

"Hmmm. You'll see."

She smiled again and walked away. That morning I had my first fried egg, over easy, and it was delicious. Over the course of the next weeks and months, I ordered eggs prepared differently, and also different kinds of bread. I even learned about pancakes and honey-baked bread.

As I was enjoying my coffee, I observed the other diners as they ate, and what they ate. I nodded to several of them and they generally started conversations with me. They were so friendly, greeting me with *good morning* and a smile, or a nod, or they stood up to introduce themselves. It was interesting to learn who lived at the hotel and who was a traveler.

Soon Mr. Saucke appeared. I invited him to join me for a cup of coffee, but he told me he and his wife had just finished their morning coffee a few minutes earlier. He dropped me off at the high school and went on to his office. I went to check in at the principal's office. We talked for a few minutes about his expectations for the week, and he wished me success

My first hour was Algebra 1. I was so nervous that I could hardly pronounce the names of some of the students as I took the roll. I thought I was going to start my lesson right away but, instead, the hour became a question and answer period. Students asked about me and my country. I decided to spend more time telling students about their new teacher than their mathematics. It was important for them to learn about me and understand my thought processes.

The same procedure continued to some degree in my modern math and geometry classes. Fourth hour was my preparation period when I had an opportunity to catch up on my administration and prepare for upcoming classes.

Fifth hour was my lunch. I sat with teachers who, like the students, also wanted to know more about me. They were very friendly. I quickly learned that the dominant group was composed of coaches and other sports-minded individuals. They talked about the latest football games and coming games at the high school, college, and national levels.

I returned to my classroom after lunch. Somewhat to my surprise, I found myself welcoming students who had large eyes and big smiles on their faces, taking in every physical inch of their new teacher from another world. It seems that word already had spread rapidly that math classes were going to be different as of today.

With this attitude of the students, I felt more confident and secure. My classes that afternoon were like those in the morning. After my last hour I gave a big sigh of relief. My first day had been successful.

The second day was more challenging. When I tried to work on my regular lesson plans, I found that most of the students simply did not know what they were doing. They could hardly solve simple problems. One student raised his hand and asked if it was possible for me to start their subject lesson from the beginning. I thought it was a legitimate request and, for the sake of the whole class, I decided to try it. But first, I asked them to be very patient with me and listen closely because my strong accent. I was amazed how much impact that statement must have had; they were very attentive whenever I lectured.

I became more and more confident of my capabilities with each day because my students behaved like angels. They did their work constantly and conscientiously. Whenever they did not understand what I was explaining, they asked questions right away.

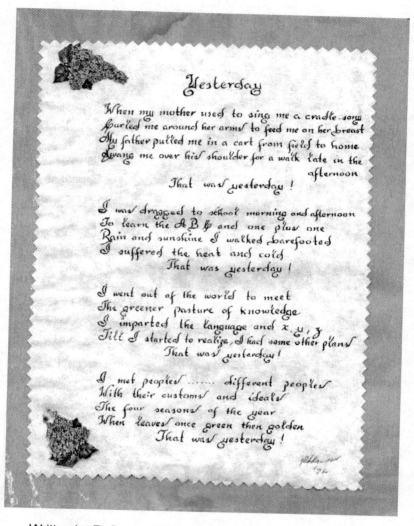

Yesterday

When my mother used to sing me a cradle song
hurled me around her arms to feed me on her breast
My father pulled me in a cart from field to home
swung me over his shoulder for a walk late in the
　　　　　　　　　　　　　　　　afternoon
　　　　　　That was yesterday !

I was dragged to school morning and afternoon
To learn the A B C and one plus one
Rain and sunshine I walked barefooted
I suffered the heat and cold
　　　　　That was yesterday !

I went out of the world to meet
The greener pasture of knowledge
I imparted the language and x, y, z
Till I started to realize, I had some other plans
　　　　That was yesterday !

I met peoples .... different peoples
With their customs and ideals
The four seasons of the year
When leaves once green then golden
　　　That was yesterday !

Written by Rufino in 1972 and dedicated to Mom and Dad

55

The Lessons of Democracy

There were occasional moments of concern, however. I was teaching before an attentive class one morning when a student I shall call Clarie persisted in talking softly in the back of the room. I deliberately stopped talking, leaned against the side of my desk, and looked in her direction. Gradually, the students turned their heads in Clarie's direction. One student suggested that she stop talking.

"Why should I stop talking?" she asked pleasantly, turning toward me. "Don't you understand that you're in a democratic country now."

"What do you mean by a democratic country?" I asked with a smile. The class sat up as a body. Something different was happening and they didn't want to miss any of the action.

"We have freedom of the press, religion, speech, et cetera," she responded.

"And that freedom applies to each of us?" I inquired.

"Yes, it does," she replied.

"Well, then, Clarie, would you please come to my desk with your books, notebooks, and personal belongings."

Clarie hesitated and then came forward with all her possessions. There was a look more of curiosity than defiance on her face. She was a nice young lady who just had a lot to say during classroom time.

"Please stand by the door," I requested. Clarie moved to the door, holding her belongings. The class was quiet.

"Since I am in a democracy," I said, "and incidentally, the Philippines is a democratic country also, would be it all right if I exercised my freedoms?"

Clarie hesitated, not sure what was happening. Other teachers hadn't called her up to the head of the classroom when she talked during lesson time.

"I guess so," she said with some doubt showing in her voice.

"Thank you," I said. "Since this is a democratic room and I am free to conduct my classes in a manner that will result in the best learning atmosphere for students..."

I paused to let every student consider what might come next. There was silence for at least ten seconds.

"...and since you're talking while I'm teaching is not conducive to learning, you are free to leave the room."

I smiled at Clarie and waited. She considered her options for a moment or two and then opened the door and left. I resumed my explanation of the problem we had been considering earlier.

When the bell rang to end the class, one student hung back as the others left the room.

"Thank you for giving us a lesson in democracy, Mr. Licos," he said. "Clarie talks a lot in other classes, too. Everyone likes her – but she just has a lot to say. I think we all learned something this morning."

My next period was preparation time for other classes. I was sitting alone in my home room when a voice over the paging speaker asked me to come to the principal's office. When I walked in, I saw Clarie sitting in the principal's office. Mr. Shriver beckoned to me. Clarie was looking down at her hands folded in her lap.

"Clarie came in to tell me what took place in your classroom a few minutes ago, Mr. Licos," the principal began. "She is quite a young lady. She didn't want to complain; she wanted to explain her position and ask what she should do in order to get back into your class tomorrow. We had a nice chat about how democracy includes respecting the rights, wishes, and needs of everyone and not just certain individuals within a group."

"Mr. Licos," Clarie broke in, unable to contain herself. "I'm sorry for speaking to you as I did. I should not have been talking while you were teaching. That was disrespecting you."

I sat down next to her.

"Clarie, nothing you said was wrong. You brought up some good points about democracy. Too many people like to quote the *freedoms from* words in the Constitution, but they don't understand that one of the most powerful freedoms is to respect and be respected by others. I always will respect your talking in class when you're on topic and contributing to your knowledge, your classmates' knowledge, and my learning about democracy in the United States."

"May I return to class tomorrow?" Clarie asked, looking at me with great earnestness.

"Of course you may," I replied with a smile. "You're already a good student – even with your talking – and I suspect you have the capability of becoming the best student in the class. Please do come back and we'll continue to explore the values of democracy together."

Clarie was in class the next day.

"Mr. Licos," she said as the students settled into their chairs. "Mr. Licos, I've decided not to talk while you're teaching today. Is that all right, sir?"

There was general laughter. I joined in.

"I appreciate your consideration," I spoke. "To what do I owe this great honor?"

There was more laughter and heads turned toward Clarie.

"When we talked after class yesterday," she said, "you emphasized the need in a democracy for everyone to respect the words and actions of others. Sometimes that's awfully difficult to do, but I'm going to try."

I thought she was finished and I was about to speak.

"But," she continued, "its almost impossible to respect some of the theorems and equations you throw at us every day. That's going to be the real challenge."

It took awhile to calm down the class, and we all had a good time talking about democracy for a few minutes before returning to mathematics. Clarie and I became good friends, and I'm certain her lesson in democracy helped her through the years.

Days, weeks, and months sped by. I became more familiar with the students, their parents, teachers, administrators and, especially, the community. Winter was approaching too fast. The wind was getting colder and the days were getting shorter. Mr. Saucke and Mr. Schriver were trying to convince me to sign my contract for the year so I would start to get paid.

Mr. Saucke picked me up at the hotel on a fall Saturday and escorted me through all the clothing stores in the city, helping me select winter clothing since I had none at all. We also visited furniture stores. He spent more than one hundred dollars on clothes for me out of his own pocket just on that day. I paid him back when I received my first two paychecks. That afternoon, he and Mr. Schriver convinced me to sign my contract for the year.

My First Snowfall

In November 1968, the class was working on a geometry problem when a student called my attention to the window. I turned and looked and, for the first time other than in a movie, saw snow falling to the ground.

"Go outside and feel the snow," my students encouraged me. I could not resist the temptation. I gave the class some additional problems to solve and asked them to keep quiet.

Outside in the chilly 25-degree weather, I stretched out my hands and experienced the strange feeling of snow falling on my skin. Then I lifted my face toward the sky and snow fell on my cheeks. What a delicious experience. I stuck out my tongue and felt the snow enter my mouth. I tried to keep my eyes open but the large, white flakes were falling too fast and my eyes instinctively closed. I bent down and scooped up a small amount of flakes on the ground. Rubbing them on my face and hands, I discovered that snow is not so cold as one might expect.

When I returned to my room a few minutes later, the students watched me intently without saying a word.

"It must seem strange to you that a twenty-eight-year-old man gets such pleasure from standing in the snow," I said. "We have no snow in the Philippines and I have seen it only in movies. This has been quite an occasion for me."

The class laughed and congratulated me on the experience. I asked them if they had completed their work and they confessed that they all had stood by the windows and watched me outside in my first taste of snow. That was time far better spent, they agreed.

"You looked like a young kid," one of my students commented.

Rufino experiencing the feeling of snow for the first time.

Settling in My New Home

Richland Center is located between two large cities; a two-hour drive south to Madison, the capital of Wisconsin, and a two-and-a-half-hour drive northwest to La Crosse. It's a beautiful town of some five thousand friendly people who live in a farming area, surrounded by hills and lakes. As I walked to and from school each morning and afternoon, or strolled around the city, people greeted me with a hello or a smile. Others took a few minutes to ask questions about my home country and what I was doing in the city.

Over time I became a rather popular item in the area and very close to my students. Parents invited me to supper, especially on Friday nights. I became the adopted son of Tom and Isabel Fowell, who I called my mom and dad. Tom worked at the U.S. Post Office; Isabel was an elementary teacher. Bob Fowell, their second son, was my student in algebra and geometry classes. Mom and Dad Fowell were grateful that Bob became interested in math. Before I came to the school, Bob was not doing well in math. Once he came to my classes, he became more interested in the subject and improved tremendously.

Bob was a big kid, over six foot tall. If he knew I was coming to their house, he would hide behind the front door. When I opened the door, he would pick me up and carry me on his shoulder well into the house. I weighed only ninety-six pounds at that time.

Mom Fowell would yell: "Bob, shame on you. Be careful with Mr. Licos; you might drop him."

Mr. and Mrs. Mort Batty (he was the school board president) considered me their adopted oriental son. A third lovely couple with whom I became quite close was Mr. and Mrs. William Brown, who owned a clothing department store. The Battys and Browns regularly invited me to barbeque outings at their homes. With all this wonderful attention, it wasn't long before I felt as though I had grown up in Richland Center. I became well acquainted with almost everyone in town, students, parents, and other adults.

Sometimes, I was invited to farms in the area where I helped milk cows in the afternoon. On Saturday mornings I often found myself in the field at 5:00 a.m., beginning a long day of bailing hay. Some of the farmers tried to teach me to drive a tractor. Due to my height, I had a problem reaching the pedals unless I stuck a pillow between my back and the back of the tractor seat to set me far enough forward. I did learn to drive tractors with the pillow in place.

In the early months of 1969, I found an apartment in a house two blocks from the high school and a block from the

Richland Community Hospital. The house was owned by two older ladies, the Richardson sisters. Winifred was about eighty-six years old and Ruth was about eighty-four. I grew to love the two ladies and I treated them like my own mom. They called me their young adopted Filipino son.

Cooking in Richland Center

The first three months rent of sixty-five dollars included my heat, water, and light. That was very inexpensive when compared with costs today. My large apartment had two bedrooms, a living room, and a kitchen with a stove, refrigerator, table, and four chairs. After I lived there for six months, I found the most recent rent check I had given to my landlords in my mailbox. My 'moms' told me they could not adequately repay me for everything I did for them, so they were returning one month's rent.

Each morning when I wakened, I played some 33-rpm records of songs sung by Elvis Presley, Johnny Mathis, Paul Anka, Dean Martin, Jerry Vale, and others. I learned later that the 'moms' were up at that hour and enjoyed listening to the music. Sometimes I would leave four of the long-playing records stacked up to play after I left the house. They told me they enjoyed the long concerts.

I fell into the habit of buying groceries for them since they no longer drove a car. I also took them shopping in Madison after I bought my first car. On one wintery day, we drove to Spring Green's ski resort, a relatively short twenty miles southeast of Richland Center.

"We didn't have these wonderful adventures when we were younger," they told me.

Every Sunday afternoon, Winnie, Ruth, and their friend who lived across the street, brought popcorn, cheese, apples, and soda to my apartment and watched the Lawrence Welk Show on my colored TV. Mr. Welk was the leader of a wonderful band that played sweet-sounding songs and had nice dancers. The ladies occasionally danced to waltzes, even though they hardly could stand up.

My 'moms' invited me to eat with them every weekend and sometimes on week nights. Now and then, I would cook Filipino cuisine – chicken and pork adobo, marinated baked chicken, egg rolls, and pancit. Pancit is a tasty Filipino dish that combines cooked rice noodles, browned chicken and pork, cabbage, carrots, onions, and shrimp. Ruth and Winnie learned to enjoy my cooking, especially the flavored dishes that included rice. When their sons, daughters, and other relatives came to visit them, I was asked to cook for them.

I met Dave Hollenbeck during my short stay at Park Hotel. He attended school at the University of Wisconsin extension at Richland Center campus. When I moved to my apartment, he occasionally brought his classmate friends to eat supper at my place. They loved my Filipino cooking. Dave eventually moved in with me while he finished his two years at the campus. He was very helpful around the apartment, washing the dishes and vacuuming twice a week while I did the cooking.

When I bought my first automobile, the Richardsons were kind enough to put in a cement patio behind the house so I could park off the street. They were the best older ladies I came to know in those years.

Learning About America

The second year in Richland Center was as memorable as the first. In the month of April, I was invited to be a judge for the Miss Kikapoo Center Beauty Pageant, twenty-eight miles northwest of Richland Center. Events such as these helped me to experience more of the leisure activities that make the United States such a exciting country.

My circle of Filipino friends living in America widened during the next years. I visited frequently with Dr. and Mrs. Parong and their two daughters in New Lisbon, forty-five miles north of Richland Center. They and another Filipino teacher, Wivina de Guzman, were my frequent visitors. I met Wivina at a teacher's convention and we soon became great friends.

Recognizing the pleasure and value of my dancing performances in becoming known in my community, I concentrated my non-teaching efforts on introducing Filipino dancing and other culture to American audiences. Gradually, I became quite well known for my performances at civic and community events. At some events I was the guest speaker as well as the dancing entertainment.

During that same summer, I enrolled at The University of Wisconsin-Platteville, fifty miles southwest of Richland Center and near the Mississippi River. The trip took an hour each way, but the time was well worth the value. When winter came along, I learned to ski at Spring Green.

In Platteville, I met the Doctor family, visiting them often and sharing lunch or supper in their house, especially when I stayed at the campus housing. Later, we met again in Madison through the Philippine American Association of Madison and Neighboring Areas (PAMANA) organization. when they moved to the state capital with their seven children.

Going Home to Mom

Early on the morning of January 9, 1972, I was startled to receive an overseas call from the Philippines. When I lifted the receiver to my ear, my oldest brother, Artemio, greeted me and said he had some difficult news. My heart started beating heavily.

"What difficult news?" I asked, my voice already shaking.

"Rufino, I'm sorry to have to tell you that Mom has died."

My throat constricted, my head began to spin, and I sat down heavily on the nearest chair. It had not occurred to me that Mom would ever die. I think that most children expect their parents simply to go on and on.

"What happened? Was she in an accident?"

My voice sounded queer to me, as though it wasn't I who was speaking.

"She died from a stroke, Rufino, quickly and without pain."

Artemio and I continued to talk for a few minutes, and I told him I would come home for the funeral. When I replaced the receiver on the telephone base, I sat in the chair for quite some time with my eyes closed, picturing Mom smiling at me as she so often did. Tears rolled down my cheeks as I realized I would never again see her smile or hear her talking to me.

I pulled myself together and went to school. When my co-workers heard the news, they advised me to go back home for the day and prepare to fly to the Philippines. They offered to have someone stay with me, but I declined with thanks. Pulling my visa and passport from a file in my desk, I was horrified to see that both had expired.

Allan Schaefer, who taught with me at Richland Center High School and had become a very close friend, stepped in to help me. He and his wife, Betty, often invited me to their home for supper, especially on weekends. They had three sons: Mike, Bill and Pat, and a daughter Sarah.

Pat was the youngest boy. He had very blonde hair and people would kid me about having a blonde son when he and I walked around downtown. The Schaefers also brought me with them whenever they visited Allan's parents and brothers in Adam, Minnesota. When Sarah was baptized I became one of her sponsors.

Now Allan gave me a lesson in American democracy by leading me through the steps to contact one of our two U.S, senators, William Proxmire, who had an office in Richland Center. Fortunately, he was in Wisconsin rather than at his Washington, D.C. office, and I immediately went over and explained my situation to him.

The senator was kind enough to call the Philippine Embassy in Chicago and explain that I needed to go home on an emergency trip. He told an embassy employee that I would be in their office the next day to renew my passport and visa. The embassy agreed to process the request on an emergency basis. I thanked Senator Proxmire profusely, and returned home to finish packing.

Later that day, a heavy snowstorm threatened to hinder my plans, but the emergency snow removal crews did their work well and cleared my path to Chicago. I returned to school the next day and learned that Allan Schaefer already had booked me to leave from Dane County Airport in Madison on the following morning. He told me to pick up my plane ticket at the airport, and handed me a letter from Senator Proxmire that I was to present at the Customs office explaining the reason for my hasty trip. I thought that was especially thoughtful of his office.

The school gave me a two-week leave of absence and sent me off to Madison. It was a nice feeling to find out how many wonderful friends I had in America. Nevertheless, my trip to the Philippines was not at all fun. My heart was heavy all the way home. I kept picturing Mom as I so clearly remembered her. I simply could not believe that she was gone from me.

When I arrived at the MIA Airport in the Philippines, I took a connecting thirty-minute flight to Baguio City, the summer capital. From there, I took a taxi cab to my home town. Dad, my two brothers, and their families met me at the door. Dad stepped out to meet me with tears rolling down his cheeks. He gave me a hug and whispered, "Your mom is gone." I couldn't whisper a word; my heart was too heavy.

It is a custom in the country that the body is kept at home until the burial day. We decided to hold the internment two days after my arrival because the longer the presence of the body, the worst pain we all felt. It was one of the saddest moments in my life. Even the opportunity to see family and friends after four years in America was not joyful enough to ease my overwhelming sadness.

I decided to continue my graduate studies in 1972. With a good deal of sadness, I recognized that I would have to leave Richland Center because of the long driving distance (one hundred and ten miles each way) to the UW-Whitewater campus. Waterloo High School, only thirty-two miles from Whitewater, was seeking a teacher, and I accepted a position there.

When I gave my letter of resignation letter to Mr. Saucke, neither he nor the school board wanted to release me, but they eventually sent me a letter of appreciation and gratitude for my services to Richland Center High School, the students and the community. My two 'moms' were shocked that I would be leaving the area and they would lose their oriental son. Both area radio stations and the *Richland Courier* announced my move to Waterloo High School, and my friends gave me a big party at the Richland Center Park before I left.

Resolution of Appreciation

For the contribution and service that Rufino Licos has made to our community during his stay in Richland Center, Wisconsin

Be it resolved that the electors of Joint School District #2 go on record this evening to express our appreciation for the contribution Mr. Licos had made to the students in our school system, the system in general, and also the community at large.

□ He has brought a refreshing attitude of respect and responsibility into his classroom.

□ He has earned the trust and understanding and admiration of his students and their parents.

□ He has tutored, without fee, many students who were having hard times academically.

□ He has spent uncounted hours assisting the Boy Scout program in Richland Center.

□ He has worked hard to assist in raising funds for our foreign exchange student program.

□ We appreciate the exposure he has given to our community of the culture of his native country.

Our best wishes for success and fulfillment at your new school in Waterloo, Wisconsin. Be assured that your personality and your talents will earn you a place of respect and high esteem in your new surroundings.

Signed,

Mort Batty, School Board President
June 1972

Chapter 4: Waterloo

Waterloo, Wisconsin, population about 3,000, has a long record of being mistaken for Waterloo in Iowa, which is below Minnesota and one state to the west of Wisconsin. Waterloo in Wisconsin is at the center of four other small towns: Columbus to the north, Watertown to the East, Lake Mills to the South, and Marshall to the West.

When I moved from Richland Center to Waterloo in 1972, Leroy Breitkreutz was the school superintendent and George Haffeman was the high school principal. Both men were great administrators, and each helped me become well acquainted with the town and school communities. I taught math, English and Spanish during my first three years. Five years later, I concentrated on teaching Spanish.

Waterloo had a bustling business community. Perry Printing (later to become a division of the company that owns *The Milwaukee Journal*), Mackay Nursery, the Van Holten pickle factory, the Malt, and a large shoe factory. In the heart of the town were three clothing stores, Zimbric Pharmacy, a bowling alley, bakery, Jim's cheese store, Dean's Meat Locker, the Waterloo municipal building, Fire Department, Arena- Anderson Dental Clinic, bowling lanes, Waterloo Clinic, and several taverns.

It was a good town for its size. Still, however, I generally left Waterloo on Friday afternoons to enjoy the weekend dancing in Milwaukee, sixty-five miles to the east, returning on Sunday evening to prepare for my next week's classes.

Waterloo families were very friendly and supportive, just as I had found the families in Richland Center. Students were respectful. When they saw me park my car in front of the school each morning, they lined up in the lobby and gave me a hug or handshake. Just as they did in Richland Center, the students let me go in line first during lunch time. Some waited for me and hugged me as I went to the cafeteria. Two of the bigger boys often would pick me up by my arms and carry me to the front of the line.

"Pave the way for Mr. Licos," they would call out, and everyone would laugh to see their teacher being escorted to the front of the line with his feet well off the floor.

After I was finished eating, boys often came to the teachers' lounge to get me to play basketball with them in the gym.

They even brought my tray back to the cafeteria so that we could play basketball longer. At times they formed a team or just played a game called 'horse'. They always were very good kids.

I frequently received hugs in the hallways from students. At the same time, my students knew when to settle down. I remained smiling.

In the winter, when the river on the park froze, students picked me up at my apartment to go ice skating with them Fortunately, I was able to take shelter in a warming house at the riverside when it got too cold. Some students were considerate enough to bring a small pillow for me to protect my rear whenever I fell on the ice.

During the summer, students invited me to play tennis at the park. Once in awhile I also played with my co-teachers. All these activities made my stay at Waterloo most enjoyable.

Rufino balancing glass at luau.

I became involved with several extracurricular activities in school and the community. I was the AFS and Spanish Club advisor and got involved with drama, the yearbook, and sports. In the community, I

Boy Scout Wood Badge training in the Philippines in 1966. Rufino is on the far right.

joined the U.S. Junior Chamber of Commerce (Jaycees), taught catechism at St. Joseph's Catholic Church, and was an international representative for the local Boy Scout troop. I joined a bowling league during the winters, and I sometimes judged cheerleading tryouts.

My Jaycees involvement took a considerable amount of time in 1973. My primary function was to head up the luau, the organization's major fund-raising activity that summer.

Preparation was demanding, but the result was a truly authentic luau. Every committee member gave unconditional support and cooperation to the project.

Fortunately, I had been very involved in the Philippine Dance Troupe of Milwaukee, and I invited them to perform with me at the luau. It was a highly successful fund-raising activity for the Jaycees.

When the Jaycees were recognizing its activities that fall, I was honored by being named the outstanding

Silahis Dance Troup performs at the Waterloo Luau in the summer of 1973.

chairman of the luau and for putting together an outstanding community service. At about the same time, I became involved in running the Miss Waterloo Pageant.

I was honored to be named the outstanding young educator of the Waterloo School District in 1974. It was quite an experience, and it gave me an opportunity to meet different people from a number of walks of life.

Even though I was making friends throughout Waterloo, I had never forgotten the kind gentleman who helped me at Los Angeles International Airport during my first day in California.

It was almost five years later that I came across the slip of paper with the man's name and address on it.

My community dancing activities took me often to Milwaukee. On one of those occasions in 1973, I found the man's house and parked across the street. For several minutes I debated whether to knock on the door. I wasn't certain he would recognize me or remember the occasion.

I remained hesitant as I walked up the walk to the front door and put my finger on the doorbell. A full ten seconds later,

I pressed the button and stepped back to await whatever might happen. Nothing happened. I was about to turn away when I thought I heard footsteps inside the house.

My eyes fixed on the door as it opened slowly. There in front of me stood the man who had loaned me five dollars five years earlier in Los Angeles.

"May I help you," he asked, blocking my view into the house.

"Mr. Walters, we met five years ago in the Los Angeles airport. You loaned me five dollars and I'm here to return it to you. My name is Rufino Licos."

The words had rushed out of my mouth almost in a single breath. Mr. Walters stared at me as though he didn't believe his eyes, or ears. Five seconds, ten seconds.

"Rufino Licos," he said slowly. "Rufino Licos, yes, yes. You have an uncle in Santa Maria named Celedonio Licoscos. Now why should I remember all that after five years."

A smile spread over his face and he offered me his hand. I took it and found myself in a surprisingly strong grip. He looked directly into my eyes which pleased me since I believe that all honest people look others in the eyes when they talk.

"Come in, come in, Rufino. How nice to see you. What brings you from Santa Maria to Milwaukee?"

"I am now teaching at Waterloo High School," I replied.

We sat in the kitchen and talked over several cups of coffee. I learned that his wife had passed on a year or so ago, and that he was not in good health. He didn't really want to talk about himself, but he was most interested in learning about my life over the years.

Eventually, it was time for me to leave for the dance rehearsal and I reluctantly pushed back my chair and stood. Digging into my pocket, I brought out a five dollar bill and offered it to Mr. Walters. With a smile, he told me to put it back in my pocket.

Betty Kehl and Rufino at Waterloo Halloween dress-up day.

"You made the offer, and that's what important," he said. "Use the money for something worthwhile and think of me at that time. I'll need all your prayers to overcome my illness."

We shook hands again and I left the house. Mr. Walters died shortly afterward. I'm so glad that I had an opportunity to repay my small debt. Unpaid debts leave an unsavory taste on one's life.

Off to Spain

Since I was teaching Spanish, I decided it was appropriate to organize a trip to Spain during the 1974 spring break. Eight students joined me on a visit to Costa del Sol in Spain on the Mediterranean Sea. Even though it was my first trip to Europe, the school administrators and parents were very supportive of my capabilities to keep the students safe. The parents shared the cost of insurance.

Six months before the trip, we helped to defray expenses through fund raising. We were able to raise one hundred twenty dollars for each of the participating students. The parents drove us to Chicago and picked us up ten wonderful days later. Several groups from other states met us at O'Hare International Airport in Chicago.

We flew from Chicago to Madrid in a nine-hour trip. We then took another flight to Costa del Sol and checked into the La Playamar Hotel close to the ocean. The hotel was surrounded by three swimming pools. We either swam in the sea or took our relaxing morning or afternoon swim in the warn water of the pool. On the first days, we traveled around the area by bus or taxi. At first, I accompanied the students everywhere – stores, restaurants, and neighboring towns, but later I let them go by themselves or in groups.

I had only one young man in the group. He was most helpful in areas where the masculine touch was important. We had gone through a short orientation about the trip before we left Wisconsin, and that introduction also proved to be most beneficial. The students were most cooperative and helpful with each other.

We took side trips to Granada, Alhambra, Cordoba, Malaga, and Mirabella, visiting old castles, churches, and other wonderful sites. We also went by boat across the Mediterranean Sea to Tangier in the Kingdom of Morocco. That trip was especially challenging for me. Initially, I was prohibited from entering Tangier because I was the only non-American in the group. I attempted to negotiate with the customs officers, but they were very strict about whom they allowed to enter. They finally relented when I told them I was the teacher and guide for my eight students. I warned them that if I was not allowed to accompany my students, they would have to give me a letter stating that they would be responsible if anything happened to my students while I was not with them. Finally, they stamped my passport and I was able to continue with the group.

We enjoyed the whole day we spent in Tangier where camels were our taxis. We were welcomed with a luncheon. The food was different, but we enjoyed every bit of it. After lunch we visited the kasbahs that contained their dark but authentic cave-like shopping stores. I asked my students if they would like to try to take a ride on a camel taxi. They at first hesitated due to the kind of streets or roads they had. Eventually, I called for one of their useful taxis that had a placard hanging by its saddle, and we took a brief ride.

Rufino on 1995 student trip to Paris with Kristi Prezak-Helper and Kathie Holz Knoke Grunwald

We relaxed on the beautiful beaches, toured the hotels, and basked in the warm weather of Costa del Sol. The students swam, strolling by the seashore, and went shopping. They had ample opportunities to practice their Spanish in restaurants, taxis, and while shopping. We also watched a bull fight. My students initially thought bull fighting was inhumane, but when we attended a second fight, they went so far as to bring along a white handkerchief to wave when the matador killed the bull.

Another event we enjoyed was the Easter Procession Celebration in Malaga, Spain. While watching the long procession, several teenage boys started talking in Spanish about the girls in my group, unaware that I understood and spoke Spanish. The boys were admiring the beautiful blonde, brunette, and light brown colors of the girls' hair.

"I wish I could run my fingers through the hair of one of these beautiful ladies," one boy said to his friends. They all smiled at the thought.

"Young men, be careful," I cautioned in Spanish. "These are my students..and they do understand some Spanish."

The boys apologized and asked my nationality. When I told them I was from the Philippines, they remarked that they thought I was Japanese. They then asked more about the girls and my students had an opportunity to speak with them. It was a good example for the students of how knowing a second language can be beneficial.

An event the students will never forget was the welcome party given by our host of the tour on Wednesday night, especially the music provided by the Los Tunos band. and the nonalcoholic sangria drink they provided to all groups.

Toward the end of the trip, I was asked to participate in a Flamingo dance on stage with a beautiful and petite Spanish girl. Fortunately, I was familiar with the Flamingo heel movements and hand clapping. I surely did not put the Wisconsin group to shame. The students cheered at the top of their voices and my group was very proud of me. That event was my first unforgettable experience in Spain.

During my twenty-four years at Waterloo High School, I organized and led five trips to Europe with students. One of the most ambitious undertakings was organized with the help of French teacher Kristi Prezak-Helper for nineteen Spanish and French students during the 1995 Spring break.

Rufino with Kristi Prezak-Helper in Madrid - 1995

Kathie Holz Knoke Grunwald, the librarian, came along with us since we had so many male and female students.

We flew from Chicago to Paris, remaining there for four days. The city and countryside were most interesting, but everything was expensive. Our hotel was very small and very expensive. Nevertheless, we had a great time visiting some gorgeous palaces, the Eiffel Tower, and many other sites.

At the Hard Rock Café, I ordered a cheeseburger, salad, french fries, and a soda. The price was a phenomenal twenty-two dollars. After eating my salad and fries, I dug into the hamburger. Much to my surprise, there was neither a hamburger patty nor cheese between the bun. When I mentioned this situation, everyone laughed, thinking I was joking. I called over the waitress and explained the situation. She carefully examined the bun for traces of hamburger or cheese and then called for the manager. He also examined the bun, apologized, and told the waitress to bring out a fresh cheeseburger. He said the meal would be free as his way of apologizing for the error.

"This can happen only once in a million times," he told us, adding under his breath, "I hope."

From Paris we took a train to Barcelona in the northeast sector of Spain, stopping at some old castles on the way to break the monotony of the train trip. Once in Barcelona, we toured the city and swam in the Mediterranean Sea. The ladies particularly enjoyed strolling along the seashore and, surprisingly, none of us was stunned to see some Spanish ladies sunbathing topless.

Barcelona was much cleaner than Paris and the hotels were a lot cheaper even though the rooms were larger and cleaner. After a two-day visit, we boarded a train and went to the capital city of Madrid, located in the center of the country. Madrid was such an enchanting city. The hotels were very tall and the rooms and bathrooms had wall-to-wall marble. Our food and transportation were fairly inexpensive. We also used the subway train to visit ordinary places and extraordinary palaces. Everything in Madrid was exciting. No other city on the tour compared with Madrid.

On our flight home from Madrid to Chicago, everyone was tired and slept most of the way. The parents met us at O'Hare International Airport in Chicago and drove us the last one hundred forty miles back to Waterloo.

When we returned to Wisconsin, we agreed that combining the French and Spanish class students was a good idea. French students were able to practice their French, and Spanish students were able to practice their Spanish. At the same time, they all had an opportunity to see two countries.

Citizen Licos

On a Friday afternoon in December 1973, I was particularly excited as the final school bell rang because I would be driving to Milwaukee to practice Philippine dances and be with my friends. As I stood in the school lobby, I felt honored that many students were cheering for me, wishing me a successful weekend, and cautioning me to drive carefully since they knew I was heading for Milwaukee.

Suddenly, my elation turned to fear as extreme dizziness overcame me and I felt that the whole world was spinning. Without being able to control myself, I threw up in the lobby and students began to panic. Some students went to look for a teacher; others ran to the office. Soon teachers and students were around me wondering what was happening.

I lived close to the school and a co-teacher drove me home. I rested for awhile but the dizziness and throwing up continued. The teacher, who had remained with me, took me to Columbus Hospital where one physician proclaimed with a smile that I was sick due to too much partying. Other doctors and nurses examined me to determine the cause of my condition and also found nothing wrong.

They examined me thoroughly in the hospital and couldn't find anything wrong with me. I requested to be transferred to a Madison Hospital for more checking since my headache, dizziness, and vomiting never stopped. After three days at Columbus Hospital, Dr. Garman referred me to Madison General Hospital where I was examined by several specialists who failed to determine the cause of my condition.

All the examinations found no cause for my condition and some of the staff wondered if I might be suffering from mental stress. I was furious when a psychiatrist appeared at my hospital door.

"You know where you came in, and you know where you go out," I said sternly. He departed.

Dr. Willis McMillan, a sinus specialist, returned and re-examined me. I advised him that I had developed an allergy to dog and cat hair, pollen, wool, and dust in 1970. At one point, I was given an EKG test and a seriously painful spinal tap to determine if I might have a brain tumor.

During an examination by Dr. McMillan on December 12, 1973, he discovered that I had a severe sinus infection. I was taken immediately to the operating room, where I was asked if I preferred to be put to sleep or remain awake. I elected to remain awake.

My nose and ears were frozen and I watched the operation on a circular mirror suspended on the ceiling. I remained in the hospital overnight, and Dr. McMillan came in the following day to remove the cotton he had placed in my nose after the surgery. I already felt like a new person, ready to go back into action.

Rufino becomes a citizen of the United States of America in May 1974.

During that same week, I was scheduled to take my oath for citizenship. Jerry Linke tried to take me to the Rock County Courthouse for the ceremony, but as we were riding down to the lobby level of Madison General Hospital (now Meriter Hospital), I became so dizzy that I had to return to my bed.

My oath taking was postponed until May 1974, and it was a great day when I became a citizen of the United States of America. When I returned to school after the ceremony, my strong and wonderful students carried me on their shoulders around the hallways chanting "Señor Licos is an American now."

Eppie and Rufino with his 1969 Dodge Challenger

Dad Comes to America

Juanita and Dr. John Eihlenfelt asked me to take care of their house during the winter of 1973-1974 while they enjoyed the warmer temperatures of Texas for six months. They wanted someone to look after the house and care for their beautiful plants.

When they returned in the spring, they asked me to move in with them as their companion in the house. In return for paying no rent or any utilities costs, I acted as their chauffeur, prepared their lunches or dinners, and did occasional grocery shopping. On weekends, I ate with them when I was home. They considered me their son. I enjoyed the relationship, but it didn't stop me from going to Milwaukee every Friday afternoon to be with a dance troupe I had joined.

Eppie outside Celedonio Senior's home in 1978.

When I was in grade school, I had become interested in many public school extracurricular activities as far back as I can remember, participating in school plays, math and spelling competitions, public speaking (we called it declamation), and folk dancing. During my high school years, I taught myself to balance a glass of water on my head as I performed folk dances. This was such an unusual ability that I found myself invited to perform at many town fiestas in the area.

While I was at St. Louis University, I joined the BIBAK (Benguet, Ifugao, Bontok and Kalinga) dance troupe, a student organization. I had no idea at that time that folk and acrobatic dancing would become such a vital part of my adult life and the lives of my family.

Juanita Eihlenfelt went for an errand downtown on a Saturday morning while John and I remained at home. John was eighty-two years old, retired from a long and successful career as a veterinarian.

Due to some mild strokes, he had difficulty both rising from a chair and walking. From where I was cooking lunch in the kitchen, I could see him sitting by the window where he liked to watch passing people and cars.

John lit his pipe and tried to put out the match. Apparently it dropped onto his chair, which was covered with a sheet. My first indication of danger was when I noticed smoke appearing at his side. I ran to his side and pulled him out of the chair. His pants and shirt were on fire now.

I beat out the fire with my hands, ran back to the kitchen, grabbed a container of flour from the counter, and poured the flour over the smoldering chair. When I discovered that the chair cover was removable, I took it to the kitchen sink and soaked it in water. Then I ran back to where I had placed John in the livingroom and helped him recover from the incident. I thanked God that I was at home when John decided to light his pipe. Juanita also was grateful when she came home and learned of the incident.

Dad came to visit in May of 1977 when Eppie and I were living with the Eihlenfelts in Waterloo. When we bought our house in Madison in the next year, Dad stayed there with us for awhile. He enjoyed accompanying us on our trip to Winnipeg, Canada when we visited Eppie"s parents and brother. We also visited Michigan where Dad's sister Antonina, her daughter Tina, and their family lived.

Dad's most enjoyable trip seemed to be our 1978 drive to California to see his brother Celedonio. On our way home, we visited one of his nephews in Las Vegas, Nevada. Dad enjoyed the excitement of the casinos and other entertainment centers. Equally impressive to him was the scenery both of the mountain states and the Great Plains. We devoted many evenings to sitting outside our motel and simply taking in the grandeur of this great country.

Regretfully, however, Dad did not enjoy Wisconsin winters, and he decided to return to the Philippines in November 1979. We had an emotional farewell at the airport when he left.

In May of 1983, I received an overseas telephone call from my oldest brother Artemio. He told me sadly that Dad passed away. As with the passing of my mother, the news was difficult to digest. Another chapter of my life was completed and I would never see my beloved father again.

I immediately requested a one-week leave to attend my father's funeral. Much to my surprise, I received a negative response. At my request, the school board held a closed emergency meeting and one of the members regretfully denied my request. Apparently not realizing that it requires nineteen to twenty-one hours to fly to the Philippines, the board declared that I could go home only for two days.

In an attempt to persuade the board to extend my leave for several more days, one of my co-teachers and a dear friend, Diann Skalitzky, passed a memo to the faculty asking each one to cover a class during their free time. Some of the teachers agreed to take my classes during their prep time until I got back. In spite of this effort, the board again denied my request for extended leave.

I thanked my co-teachers for their concern and gave up my trip to the Philippines. Instead, I finished the one remaining one month of school. Our three daughters, Heidi, Regina and Neri, had returned to the Islands in the early Spring and were able to visit once more with their grandfather before he passed away. Eppie and I followed as soon as the school year ended.

Purple, Pink or Polka Dotted

Diann Skalitzky became a substitute teacher at Waterloo High School in the fall of 1973 when the school had about three hundred students and a population of 2,200 citizens. It was difficult for anyone who lived in Waterloo to not know everyone else who lived in Waterloo.

Diann and Gary own one thousand acres of good farm land at the edge of the city. Gary works for the Wisconsin Department of Transportation and the couple raises pigs on a portion of their land. One of her tasks was to substitute for Rufino in algebra, English, and Spanish as needed.

She continues to teach today and she remembers her teaching days with Rufino with great fondness.

"Rufino seldom was sick, but I did substitute for him on those rare occasions."

Almost all the faculty, most of whom were single or had no children, would get together on Fridays for group dinners in those years. They became a family within themselves. At that time, male teachers received $100 more per year than female teachers because they were considered the breadwinners.

"Rufino invited my husband and me to his home for a chicken dinner that he had marinated during the day. He was living on North Monroe Street about a block and a half from school. A doctor lives there now. The dinner was absolutely wonderful.

"Rufino was very loving and concerned about the welfare of those around him. He always had students prepare family trees. He wanted students to learn about people who spoke different languages, and to learn the whole picture – how they lived, their culture, dance, food, holidays. He tried to incorporate all these elements in his teaching."

Rufino and Diann were class advisors in the mid-1980s for a trip to New Orleans during spring break – the first class trip since the 1960s. Diann's husband Gary, and the school's science teacher, Mark Geiger, accompanied them. Along the way, they stopped at St. Louis, Missouri; Springfield, Illinois; and Lincoln, Illinois, visiting President Grant's farm, the Anheuser Brewery, the Transportation Museum, and The Aviary at the St. Louis Zoo. On the return trip, they connected with Mark Twain and Tom Sawyer, coming up through Twain's home town of Hannibal, Missouri. Rufino and Diann also worked together on graduation and prom (promenade) ceremonies together.

Rufino never hesitated to help a student who needed something. He was a major promoter of the American Field Service (AFS) program at the school. AFS began shortly after the outbreak of World War I, as a group of fifteen Americans who lived in Paris and volunteered to drive ambulances for the American hospital there. By the end of the war, its size had grown to more than two thousand volunteer drivers.

Diann Skalitzky and Rufino in her classroom - 2003

The drivers were not armed since their mission was to save lives rather than take them. During World War II, American Field Service volunteers were stationed in Burma, Europe, India, North Africa, and Syria When the war ended in 1945, they pledged to

80

work toward changing the world's focus from hostility to friendship through student exchange programs that would help men and women live for short periods with families in other countries. In so doing, they would learn the values and concerns of others and build foundations for avoiding conflicts.

Exchange programs began in 1947, bringing fifty-two high school students from ten countries to the United States for a year-long exchange. More than 290,000 participants have taken part in cultural exchanges since that year. Diann recalls:

"Rufino's last student trip was to Spain and France with our librarian, Kathleen Holz Knoke Grunwald and Kristi Prazak-Hepler. He always pushed to have students see other parts of the world. He didn't believe that the world should revolve around the school, nor that students should accept Waterloo as the center of the universe. Rufino believed the school should be a vehicle to help students experience the world.

"Students didn't care whether he was purple or pink polka dotted. That he was not American born meant nothing to the students. How we loved and cared for our students was most important to Rufino. He lived through some exceedingly difficult situations with certain school administrators, but he was backed by most of the faculty and children, always concentrating on what was best for the students. He never reacted with anger, nor was he spiteful or vindictive, no matter what the outcome of disagreements with school or district policies."

Rufino enjoyed the school sports activities at Waterloo. He coached volleyball at the junior high school, directed the school's plays, and was the school's newspaper advisor for a time. He also was the scorer or timer for basketball games.

Gary and Diann continue to visit with Rufino and Eppie from time to time, often at the East Town Mall in Madison where Rufino walks daily for exercise and knows most of the merchants.

"Rufino has a fondness for pig meat. We have a large hog farm. My father-in-law was moving pigs around one day when three 100-pounders got loose, ran onto

81

the road, and were hit by cars. My son and I gutted the pigs and asked Rufino if he would like one. He took all three. We've had a lot of pig cookouts together. When we had a big pork roast at our house one weekend, Rufino stuffed the pig with lemon leaves, oranges, and celery sticks."

Many of the students at Waterloo High School today (2003) remember Rufino either directly or through the stories told by their parents. They greet him with a little tap dance of the sort that he did when he taught there. He returns to the school from time to time to put on presentations in the elementary school for fine arts week.

Diann and Rufino worked well with the Mexican students who moved into the area rather than return to Mexico after the harvest season. Health courses were mandated by the state. Diann taught the health classes with the help of Rufino's knowledge of the students' native language. The two teachers teamed up to help students learn English and health at the same time. She would take pictures from an old health book and write out body parts in English. Rufino then would write the parts in Spanish.

"Rufino was my savior. We had kids coming to our school who understood no English at all. Rufino would translate our exams into Spanish. The students then had to answer the questions in English. He could talk to them in Spanish and correct their Spanish as well as teach them English. He would have an opportunity to work with these children for two or three hours a day."

"Rufino is remembered lovingly and with a smile. He would become upset and speak in a harsh manner to any student who hurt someone else, either physically or mentally. He never tried to stop physical aggressiveness with force; his style was to talk persuasively with the students involved, and he almost always was successful. He was known as "The Hugger" by the students and faculty. Students would come up and give him big bear hugs. They still do it today when he returns for a visit."

After Rufino and Eppie married and moved to Madison, Eppie became as much of a beloved figure at Waterloo High School as was her husband. She attended all the dance recitals, and she taught others to sew, demonstrating her techniques by creating satin costumes and other clothing items.

Cooking has never been Eppie's favorite task. In the years that Rufino's in-laws lived in Wisconsin while the children were growing up, they did whatever cooking Rufino left to them. Eppie helped with the wash, sharing the obligations of a working family. There always was time to attend various school presentations, however. His dad also attended many of the functions, as did Eppie's mother and father during their visits to the Midwest.

For four or five years, Rufino, Diann, Dennis Baker, and Lynette Reinfeldt ate lunch together in the home economics room. Those were the days when smoking was allowed in the teachers' lounge and none of the four smoked. They ate whatever others contributed on any day.

"Rufino always offered the most creative menus. I ate everything he presented except a Filipino meal of half-hatched eggs (called balot)."

During his middle years, Rufino continued to look much younger than he was. He was in his thirties when he was required to show his identification card at the Playboy Club and Miller Stadium proving that he was older than twenty-one.

When Rufino's father died, Diann lined up substitutes for one full week to cover Rufino's time away for the funeral, but the administration would not allow sufficient time, in his opinion, from his teaching duties for him to fly to and from the Philippines and mourn with the family and friends.

Rufino elected to take early retirement from Waterloo in May 1996. The lure of teaching remained too strong, however, and he became a substitute teacher at DeForest Middle and High School on the outskirts of Madison a short time later. He continues to teach at DeForest at this writing in 2003.

In all his teaching years, Rufino felt that only one small group of school administrators treated him differently from other faculty members because he was Filipino. In all other locations, his background and nationality were considered an asset for students and faculty to draw upon to learn more about cultures around the world.

God never left Rufino alone during his teaching years in the late 1980s. When the Columbus school system learned that he was a part-time teacher at Waterloo High School and could use additional teaching time, the superintendent asked him to help with their Spanish program. For the next two years, Rufino drove thirty miles each morning to teach two classes in Columbus, then drove twenty miles to Waterloo to teach five additional classes. He then traveled another twenty-five miles to his home in Madison. After two years, when the Waterloo school district realized that Rufino was teaching five periods each day, he was reinstated as a full-time teacher under the terms of the school's master contract.

"It was difficult for me to leave Columbus High School because the students were so much fun to teach and the teachers were very supportive and helpful to me," Rufino says. "However, I certainly appreciated returning to an easier driving schedule each day."

Chapter 5: Romance in the Air

When I emigrated to the United States in 1968, Eppie's Aunt Marcelina Preposi, who was a teacher and had been a good friend since my high school years, gave me Eppie's address in Canada. She suggested that some day I might visit Eppie, who had completed pre-nursing school at the Far Eastern University in Manila and the nursing program at St. Rita Hospital School of Nursing in Manila. In 1967, she accepted a position at Dauphin General Hospital, Dauphin, Manitoba as a nurse. Seven years later, she joined the staff as general duty nurse at the Health Sciences Center in Winnipeg, Manitoba, Canada.

Eppie subsequently continued her nursing career at Mercy Hospital in Janesville, Wisconsin and Methodist Hospital (which later became Meriter Hospital) in Madison, Wisconsin.

Shortly after I began my teaching career in Richland Center, I wrote to Eppie and we established an international correspondence that lasted for several years.

Eppie at work in 1970

Eventually, Eppie and I married, and we have lived a wonderfully happy life ever since. But the road to the altar was bumpy. The major hurdle was that when I left the Philippines, I had an understanding with a young Filipino lady. When I flew home in 1972 for my mother's funeral, I learned that my marriage was expected to take place the next year.

Before I returned to the States, my fiancée asked me to leave behind one of my worn T-shirts. This worried my dad because some Filipinos believe that a person can use a worn T-shirt to spill bad luck on the owner. As it happened, after I returned to Wisconsin, I felt it would be best if she and I did not marry. I wrote and told her my decision. To my knowledge, she never applied that curse, and I don't know to this day what happened to the T-shirt.

When I transferred to the Waterloo School District in 1972, I became involved with a dance troupe in Milwaukee where I got to know a very nice young lady who was a friend of my Uncle Bonifacio and Auntie Luz in Milwaukee. Over time, our friendship developed into a more serious relationship and I became concerned that she was in a rush to marry. Having just broken off one engagement, I was leery of establishing another potentially long-term relationship.

At about that same time, I received a letter from Eppie in which she congratulated me on my pending marriage in the Philippines. She wanted to know the name of the lucky girl and how many children we already had. I immediately wrote back and explained the situation. Soon afterward, Eppie and I entered into a serious relationship that blossomed into our long and happy marriage.

Eppie at age 15 during high school Junior Prom

Eppie sponsored her younger brother Alexander when he decided to emigrate to Winnipeg in 1970. Alex had graduated from St. Louis University of Baguio City with a specialty in accounting and had passed the tough certified public accountant exam. He was one of my boarders in the Philippines when I managed an apartment for college students during the days that I taught at the University. My oldest brother Artemio was a highway engineer in the city at that time. When I moved to the United States, Artemio took over the apartment management.

Alex eventually moved to Canada and I saw him from time to time when I visited Eppie. He had married Rose Velasco, a Filipino nurse who worked in Canada.

I fell into the habit of driving to Winnipeg, the capital city of Manitoba Province, when my school year ended. I spent half the summer with Eppie, Alex, and Rose. Eppie was living with Jane, Jo, and Mhae Tano, Eppie's long-time friends from Baguio City. They provided me with sleeping quarters during my visits. In return, I prepared breakfast for all the girls on most mornings and then drove them to work and picked them up in the afternoon.

Everything has its perfect place in God's plan. Eppie's folks in the Philippines asked her if she had found someone with whom she would like to settle down. Since Eppie and I had been corresponding and seeing each other for a long time, she told her parents that she had found a man from her own town in the Philippines. She did not give them my name.

We learned later that her parents wrote down the names of all the single men from our town, but my name wasn't on the list because it was still widely believed that I was engaged.

In a subsequent letter, Eppie mentioned my name as the man she had selected. Everyone in the family back home agreed with her choice. Eppie's

Exchanging wedding vows in 1975 in Winnipeg, Canada

oldest sister Aurora, who was my classmate and graduated with me in sixth grade, voted one hundred and one percent for me, I was told.

Eppie's letter in which she wrote about me without mentioning my name happened to be included with another letter sent by her parents to Alex.

He received the package on the same afternoon that he had invited Eppie to join him for supper. She had many excuses for not being able to have dinner with Alex, but he insisted on her presence due to the content of the letter.

Alex picked up Eppie at her apartment. While they were having supper, he handed her the letter. As she looked at it, he asked for the name of the man she intended to marry. Eppie laughed and told him about me.

"I really like him," she confessed to Alex.

"I like him, too," Alex replied. "I think you should invite him to visit us this summer."

Eppie looked puzzled. "You know Rufino?" she asked.

"Yes, I know Rufino," he answered with a smile. "He rented me space in the apartment he managed when I was going to college in Baguio City. I know him well."

So it was that in the summer of 1973 that I flew to Winnipeg to meet the family. It was a happy reunion for Alex and me. During the summer of 1974, when I returned to Wisconsin, Eppie came with me. Everyone approved of her, even my landlords.

That same summer, Eppie and I became engaged while we were in Richland Center. The event was blessed by Father Reardon, the priest of St Mary's Church.

I spent a good amount of time in Winnipeg during the early summer of 1974, learning more about Eppie's friends and the city. Eppie's friends were wonderful. My soon-to-be bride and I went on picnics, walked through the beautiful parks, and attended weddings, birthdays, baptisms, and other get-togethers with friends. We even went fishing on weekends, catching lots of fish and cooking many of them at our campsite.

When the 1973-74 school year ended in the first week of

Members of the wedding party, July 5, 1975

88

June, I immediately drove to Canada. Wedding preparations were proceeding well. All the invitations had been answered. Eppie's friends held a pre-wedding dance and cocktail party for us during which the participants donated a small amount of money as an advance wedding gift.

The summer of 1974 was doubly hectic for me because I enrolled at UW-Whitewater to earn my lifetime teaching certificate, a Wisconsin state requirement. I found myself constantly driving between Wisconsin in the United States and Winnipeg in Canada, a 795-mile trip in each direction.

My schedule was so busy that I was unable to get to Whitewater (110 miles southeast of Richland Center) until the fifth week of classes. It was my good fortune that my professor allowed me to enter the classes with only

Eppie's wedding gown, made in the Philippines

four weeks remaining. I had to work twice as hard to make up the first four weeks during the same period. I thank God that I came through the course with flying colors and received my life certificate at the end of the summer in 1974.

We had set the wedding day for July 5, 1975 and I soon learned how complex wedding preparations are. There were the matters of the wedding gown, bride's maids, best man, other members of the wedding party, invitations (which we ordered from the Philippines), wedding gift lists, flowers, church arrangements, finding a priest to officiate the wedding in Canada, reception details, honeymoon details.

This was one time of many that I learned who were our true friends.

We selected the Fort Gary Hotel in Winnipeg for our wedding reception. Alex, Danny Cabatan, the Tano sisters, and several others stepped in to handle many details of the wedding.

Alex and company decorated the church, the car we rode in, the hotel, and the reception room. They even arranged a bachelor's party by the airport at a striptease bar. Every time I turned around, someone poured a drink into my glass. The result was that, little by little, I became seriously intoxicated.

Daniel offered to drive me home at four in the morning. But instead of taking me to Alex's house, he headed toward Eppie's apartment. On the way, just as we passed the legislative building, I leaned out of the car and was quite sick. I'm so glad I didn't wait until I got to Eppie's apartment. That episode taught me a good lesson about over-indulging. I did not enjoy being unable to control my actions and I never drank heavily again.

The Wedding Party. Jerry Linke, David Teiwes, Father McClowsky, Rufino and Eppie, Norma Clemente, Jane Tano, Isabel Fowell.

Sixty-five friends from Milwaukee, Waterloo, and Minnesota drove to Winnipeg to attend our wedding. They stayed in several hotels. The wedding was conducted in Filipino, American, and Canadian traditions, a nice international touch. Father McClowsky officiated.

Members of the wedding party were:

Maid of Honor: Jane Tano

Best Man: David Teiwes

Bride's Maids: Marina Tano, Corazon Espiritu, Flordiliza Eugenio, Diosa Ebora.

Ushers: Val de Jesus, Daniel Cabatan, Gerry Ganaden, Rolando Gomez, Butch Andojera.

Principal Sponsors: Tom and Isabel Fowell, Mort Batty, Jerry Linke, Norma Clemente

Candle Bearers: Josephine Tano, Oscar Carbonell.

Veil Bearers: Minerva de Padua, Mario Lito Rosario.

Cord Bearers: Amor Amante, Dannie Singalong.

Flower Girls: Iona and Athena Natividad.

Ring Bearer: Alexander Aguedo Avecilla Jr.

Organist: Miguel Igualado

Toast to the Bride: Conrado Gomez

People still speak of the wedding today. During the reception, we followed the American and Canadian custom of the groom removing a garter from the bride's thigh and throwing it to the bachelors, then throwing the bride's bouquet to the unmar-

The Avecilla family in 2001: Alex, Rose, Roselie, Almer, Alex Jr.

ried girls. Eppie and I danced alone for a moment or two until others in the wedding party joined us. A few minutes later, our guests came onto the dance floor.

As we danced, the guests observed the Filipino custom of pinning money to my suit, shirt, and clipping it in my hair and to Eppie's gown and veil. We received more than two hundred dollars during that dance.

Another custom was tossing the groom. I lay on a blanket that had been spread on the floor. Each man in the wedding party then took hold of the blanket and tossed me high into the air. Being that I weighed barely one hundred pounds at the time, I'm surprised that I didn't go through the ceiling.

After all the fun, joy, and excitement of the wedding, Eppie and I went to our suite. Much to our surprise, and frustration, some of our friends had turned our mattresses upside down.

Eppie and I never will forget the task of preparing the wedding bed at three in the morning when we already were exhausted.

We decided to spend the next day at another hotel to get away from everyone and enjoy our second day of marriage alone.

After a wonderful relaxing day, we were back in our suite when the telephone rang at eight in the evening. I answered it and heard loud giggles, laughing, and screaming.

"We know you're there," voices yelled at us with great laughter. Fortunately, however, the partygoers found something else to do without us for the remainder of the evening. In the morning, the telephone rang at eight o'clock. It was Father McClowsky.

"How would you like to play golf this morning?" he asked. How could I refuse! I kissed Eppie and left her sleeping. Father McClowsky and I and spent the entire morning on the golf course.

The remainder of the week was peaceful. On the weekend, friends organized a birthday party for Eppie at a nearby park.

We still were a little tired, but we enjoyed the get-together with our friends. Eppie and I decided to drive back to Wisconsin on the following weekend. Alex and the Tano sisters accompanied us to the border of Manitoba and North Dakota. Before they let us go at the check point, Eppie's former roommates called to her by her nickname:

"Paniang, you better change your life style now."

They knew more about her life style than I did, I soon found. Married life at the age of thirty-six was full of joy and adjustments for me. Eppie was thirty and also had adjustments to consider.

Rufino and Epifania Licos

We quickly learned that we had become acquainted with only some of each other's habits, likes, and dislikes during our friendship and courtship. Being a bachelor and bachelorette for so many years made adjustment to marriage more difficult, but we were up to the task because we were truly in love.

I had come to know Eppie as a neighbor and friend of the family. Whenever we had met on the street, Eppie had turned her face the other way, as was the custom when a young girl had no interest in a man.

Whenever I went to her home to play Scrabble with her brothers and sister, she never came down from her room to join us. Years later, when I was teaching in Baguio City, her Aunts Marcelina, Estang, and Dora would invite me for lunch in their apartment. On those occasions, never did Eppie come out from her room.

Eppie (second from right in back row) with her family, c1964.

Now we were married — without having done much dating nor really learning much about each other. Who were we, indeed. It required a good deal of patience from each of us, and a good amount of give and take, to adjust to a husband-wife relationship, but that was only one of the joys of marriage.

I quickly found that Eppie had seldom cooked. Since I enjoyed cooking, I took on that assignment and she accepted responsibility for washing dishes and cleaning the house. That has been our greatest division of labor. We have managed in this way throughout our marriage — twenty eight years at this writing in 2003 — and we're still a great husband and wife team, the best of friends, and the proud parents of our four lovely girls.

When we returned to the States following our wedding and visit to the Philippines, we moved in with the Eihlenfelts and remained there for two-and-one-half years before we purchased our home in Madison.

In the Spring of 1976, Eppie again went home to the Philippines to complete some requirements for her nursing board exams that she would be taking in Wisconsin. I followed her across the ocean after school closed for the summer. Thus, we celebrated our first wedding anniversary with our family and friends back home. We returned to the States in July 1976. Because there was no reciprocity for nursing certification between Wisconsin and Canada, Eppie was assigned to eight months of service orientation, beginning in August 1976, at

Mercy Hospital in Janesville, forty miles south of Waterloo. She took an apartment near the hospital.

My weekly schedule centered around driving Eppie to Janesville on Sunday afternoon, returning with cooked food on Wednesday after school, and bringing her home to Waterloo on Friday afternoon. Those eight months seemed like years. Fortunately, Eppie met some Filipino families who worked in the hospital, and

Eppie's Aunts Eustaquia, Teodora, and Marcelina

At the wedding reception

that was a great relief for me knowing that she would be looked after when she was away from me.

When Eppie completed her service orientation and returned to Waterloo, she received a position at Colonial Nursing Home in Madison. She dreaded the daily fifty mile round trip, especially in the dark.

Driving was even more difficult during the winter months. Several times she found herself in perilous situations because of fog, rain, and snow. Nevertheless, she was patient and remained with the Home until she could take the state board exam and receive her Wisconsin nursing license.

Three years later, on June 27, 1979, Eppie brought Heidi Mhae into our life. We were fortunate that Eppie's parents,

Aguedo and Caridad Avecilla, were with us at that time. Sixteen months later, on December 21, 1980, Regina Christine was born, and we appreciated Dad and Mom's help with the infants.

Neri Corine arrived on April 27, 1982, and Raechel Nichole completed our family on May 10, 1985. Our romance strengthened with the arrival of each daughter. We are blessed with four lovely, talented, and intelligent girls. Each is a precious daughter who we love dearly.

Eppie Avecilla's Family

Front: Rustica, Caridad, Aquedo, Jose;
Rear: Alexander, Eppie, Aurora, Reynaldo

Rustica is a medical doctor. Jose is a mechanical engineer. Alexander is a certified public accountant. Eppie is a registered nurse. Aurora is an elementary school teacher. Reynaldo is a business graduate.

Chapter 6: Madison

In 1978, I took an evening position as a waiter at the Zizzling Steak House on East Washington Avenue. Eppie was working the 3:00-11:30 p.m. shift at the hospital. My co-workers knew I was studying at the University to pursue my career in education. My boss, Joe Penland, also knew I was a school teacher.

The Zizzling staff immediately treated me like one of their own and we had a great time. My job was to vacuum, fill up the ketchup bottles, salt and pepper shakers when we closed for the night. Sometimes, the staff included me in routine as well as weird waiter activities, particularly when the manager left.

The Licos family in 1997

They threw various restaurant items — salt shakers, napkin holders, cups, silverware — to one another, slipped ice cubes inside their shirts or pants, and did other stunts of that nature as they were closing the restaurant each evening. I joked and laughed with them, and sometimes sang songs with them.

I became well- known to customers. They often requested me as their waiter before they came, or when they arrived.

Customers referred to me as "their little Filipino waiter", which didn't bother me at all. Most of the time my lowest tips in the four hours I worked was $95.00. On weekends, I earned as much as $160.00 in tips. Eppie and I enjoyed counting my tips when I came home.

Customers who were not assigned to my tables occasionally slipped one or two dollars into my shirt pocket when they left the restaurant to thank me for my keeping their glasses filled with water and their cups full of coffee. They appreciated every little thing I did for them and I came to understand more clearly how attention to the smallest details was important in my relations with others.

A grandma called the restaurant two days ahead of her arrival to learn if I was working that day. Her granddaughter was celebrating her sixteenth birthday and she wanted me to be their waiter. I had the pleasure in serving all twenty people at the party. Grandma called me aside before they sat down and told me she had brought a birthday cake and decorated it with sixteen candles. She requested me to bring in the cake on the top of my head with the candles lighted.

When everyone finished eating, I came out from the kitchen with the cake and sixteen lighted candles on my head and a glass of soda in each hand. Customers stopped eating to stare at me; my manager watched with some trepidation as he followed in my path.

As I reached the young celebrant, I knelt beside her and said: "Happy birthday young lady."

I handed her the glasses of soda. took down the tray holding the birthday cake, set it on the table, and the patrons throughout the restaurant applauded. One customer said in a loud voice: "Boy, we're not only getting full in here; we're also being entertained."

On one evening, I had the honor of serving Senator Gaylord Nelson and his family. The moment I sat them at a table, he asked me if I was from Hawaii.

"You could say that, sir," I answered truthfully since I had passed through that state on my initial trip to the States.

As they were eating, the senator became inquisitive about my life. I told him that I was in the United States to pursue a career in education, and that I was a senior at UW-Madison. That was not the truth, but I didn't want to tell him that I was a teacher earning so little money that I had to hold a second job. He replied that his son was a sophomore at the University.

The second time the senator came to the restaurant, he pulled me onto his lap and said to everyone around him:

"This is my Hawaiian-Oriental son."

I let that go without comment. He really was quite nice.

It was a busy weekend evening when a party of three men and three women entered the restaurant. They sat at one of the tables to which I was assigned. They were very loud and one of them swore a great deal. I thought their wives listened surprisingly patiently to their husbands. I greeted them and told them I was going to be their waiter. One of the gentlemen yelled at me: "How about bringing us a pitcher of coffee."

"Yes, sir. How many cups, sir?"

"Five, please," the lady next to the loud man said. One lady ordered a glass of water.

When I brought the drinks, the same loud-voiced man yelled at me again.

"We're ready to order now. We're starving."

"Yes, sir," I politely replied.

The three men were drunk and the loudest was the most obnoxious. At one point, he picked up a glass filled with water and, as he tried to drink, the glass slipped from his hand and dropped onto his lap.

One of the ladies sighed: "Oh, my God. Be careful. Now you're wet." She took the napkin and tried to dry him off.

"Oh s----"," he yelled in his loud voice, looking directly at me. I walked quickly to the kitchen, retrieved a cloth, and handed it to the lady who, I presumed, was his wife. The man continued to moan and swear while I took their orders and returned to the counter. Many patrons looked in my direction with pity in their eyes. I managed to smile at them as I went around refilling their cups and glasses.

"Is there anything else you need, ladies and gentlemen,?" I asked as I placed their food on the table. The loud one spoke up again.

"Salt and pepper!"

"It's on the table, sir."

"I want A1 Sauce for my steak."

His wife smiled at me.

"I'm sorry. He's had a lot to drink."

I could see on her face that she was drowning with shame.

"You must have just come from a party or a big game and you're passing through," I suggested.

"Yes, we just came from the Packers game, and they won."

"You better shut up and give me more napkins," Loudmouth demanded.

"Yes, sir," I said. I brought back some napkins. He was the most obnoxious customer I ever encountered.

"I don't think he can go to work tomorrow with the state of mind and body like that," I said, looking at his wife.

"We are from Illinois. He's a high school principal."

Loudmouth acknowledged his high station in life by picking up his cup and tipping its contents on the table.

"Son a b----," he yelled. I handed him the rest of the napkins that were in my hands. I could hold my temper no longer.

"Sir, what kind of principal are you," I said. Everyone looked at me with surprise, and it got quiet in the restaurant.

"If I were in your place, I would be ashamed of myself acting so unprofessionally in public. I don't care who you are, but in real life I am a high school teacher. I'm working here to get experience in a different walk of life. You make me ashamed of my profession."

With that statement, I walked away and took care of my other customers. Loudmouth said nothing more. Soon his wife came over to me and apologized for his behavior. I walked back with her and handed them the bill.

"We're very sorry, sir, with what happened," one of the other men said. "We're all friends, just celebrating."

With that, Loudmouth perked up and said to me:

"Young man, I am really very sorry for my actions and words. You must be a great teacher wherever you teach."

Possibly to compensate for their behavior, they left a twenty dollar bill on the table, a substantial tip in those days.

Shortly thereafter, I left the restaurant and took a position at Thrift Drug Store. I enjoyed associating with my co-workers. The manager, Wally Motyka, and his partner, Allan Suehs, were great mentors. Occasionally, my knowledge of the Spanish language allowed me to interpret for Spanish-speaking customers who needed an explanation about their medicine.

I particularly enjoyed working with Kaye Pearson, Doris Hicks, Marlene, Gina, Linda, and Suzette. After work we often would go to the Imperial Garden restaurant across the street from the mall for a drink and egg rolls.

Three years later, when the Thrift Drug Store closed, I found work at the J.C. Penney store in the men's department. Students often brought their parents and friends to Penney's to visit with me and to buy clothes. I partnered with some wonderful men and women, including Darlene Joyce and Phil

Rufino with J.C. Penney's
Phil Filz and
Darlene Joyce

Filz. We had great Christmas parties, just as we had at Thrift Drug.

After two-and-one-half years, I left Penney's because teaching was taking all my time. During this period of my life, I learned that a truly good salesperson must be courteous, kind, patient, respectful, honest, and always have a warm smile.

Antonia Yecla

Antonia came to the United States in 1998, traveling by herself. She called me on the telephone, using the listing in the Philippine Immigration Book and, in my absence, talked with Eppie. We met Antonia the next day. During that meeting, we learned that we were listed as a designated contact in the book presented by the Immigration Service to Filipinos who immigrated to Wisconsin.

Antonia asked me if I could help her find a job. She seemed reluctant to offer information about her training and education, and I assumed that she needed a "starter" position. I took her to Woodman's Grocery Store where she was hired immediately. Unfortunately, the type of work to which she was assigned was too difficult physically for her to handle, and she had to leave Woodman's after a few weeks.

Adele Licos (Rufino's niece, next to Eppie) meets with Antonia, Gladys Buenavista, and Helen Navarro during her visit to the United States.

I then brought her to a clothing store where we had a distressing meeting. When I asked the receptionist for an employment application, the woman looked carefully at us and then looked away without responding. When I asked again for an employment application, she looked coldly at me and said there were no openings at the time.

"We just want to file an application for future employment," I told her.

The woman took an application form from a drawer in the desk and slammed it and a pen on the counter without further comment. She then turned back to her work.

My blood pressure quickly rose to the near-boiling point.

"You're being rude," I said. "Why are you acting this way toward us?"

The receptionist ignored me.

"I wish to talk with the assistant manager," I told her.

Without speaking a word to us, she lifted her telephone and asked the assistant manager to come to the reception desk. Then she continued working without looking at us.

The assistant manager appeared within a minute.

"Rufino," he said with a smile, "what brings you here?"

The receptionist looked startled but continued working.

I introduced Antonia to my old friend and said she had just arrived from the Philippines and was looking for work.

"Of course, Rufino, we always have openings for people you recommend. Shirley," he said, looking at the receptionist, "take Antonia's application and schedule her for an interview tomorrow, please."

Shirley smiled and turned to Antonia.

"Please complete this application form," she said, now speaking in a friendly voice and smiling broadly at the woman who probably was going to be the company's newest employee.

"What time would be convenient for you to come in tomorrow for your interview?"

When we returned the next day, Antonia noticed that on top of the application in the manager's office was a note that said: "Be nice to her."

I later learned that Antonia has a bachelor of science degree in commerce major (equivalent to a business major in the United States). It wasn't long before she felt comfortable enough in the States to apply for a position at First Federal Bank. She was hired at the nearby East Washington branch, but she had no way to get to work because she had no driver's license at that time and she wasn't living near a bus line.

Antonia found an apartment when she started working at the bank. She went to school for driving lessons and she got her driver's license. She then bought a car. After three years at the bank she was promoted to a head teller position. At about the same time, she received her Green Card that granted her permanent residency in the United States.

The Schoenstatt Movement

The Schoenstatt Movement today has more than 180 shrines throughout the world. Each shrine is orientated to the original Christian image of community: the family as exemplified in the Holy Family of Nazareth, and united by a common bond of love and mutual respect.

Schoenstatt followers have built more than one hundred pastoral and retreat centers around the world that are visited by some two million pilgrims annually.

Licos family at fund-raising event for Schoenstatt Shrine - 2002

Schoenstatt's spiritual center is a place of the same name near Vallendar on the River Rhine, West Germany, where Father Joseph Kentenich and a small number of young men first gathered on October 18, 1914. In the Middle Ages, a monastery called *Eyne Schoene Stat* (a beautiful place) occupied the site. Today, it has become an international place of pilgrimage and spiritual life.

With more than thirty different houses for retreats and communities, churches, places of spiritual formation and religious craft workshops, Schoenstatt is one of the largest religious centers in the world.

Rufino and Eppie visit with Flora Cochingyan at the Schoenstatt Shrine in Waukesha, Wisconsin

These centers are places for reflection and prayer, for spiritual formation, and pastoral training. Whoever visits a Schoenstatt Center should feel at home, inwardly transformed, and should receive impulses for experiencing and applying faith in daily life.

Late in the 1980s, Gina's godmother, Flora Cochingyan invited us to participate in the Santa Cruzan (May Flower Festival) celebration at the Schoenstatt Shrine in Waukesha, west of Milwaukee. The annual event is held on Mothers' Day. We were asked to entertain after the mass, procession, and crowning of the Blessed Mother Thrice Admirable.

All four girls were crowned *Reyna Elena* (Queen Helena) during the Santa Cruzan before its founder, Oya (Flora), passed away in May 2002, four days after we celebrated the Festival's twenty-fifth jubilee.

The Schoenstatt Shrine in Madison is directed by Sister Mary Erlinda. She was born on April 18, 1945 of religious Filipino parents who contributed to her spiritual openness. She grew up in a good Catholic home and attended a Catholic high school in Tagudin, Ilocos Sur.

His Eminence Ricardo Cardinal Vidal at Schoenstatt Shrine in the Philippines with Myrna San Agustin (seated), Sister Erlinda, Andrea Villa, and Rufino.

God had specific plans for Sister Erlinda. She devoted ten years to teaching at a school on Staten Island (a short ferry ride from New York City), and then served for several years as the Catholic church's Director of Religious Education in New York and New Jersey.

God was guiding her path. She came to know the Schoenstatt Movement and joined the group in 1965. While "in formation" in Germany, she met Father Kentenich. She was appointed superior at Schoenstatt Heights Retreat House in Madison in 2001.

Licos daughters at the Santa Cruzan festival in Waukesha.

In February 2002, the Licos family and some Filipino friends performed at the Madison shrine over a two- day period

104

to raise money that would be used to build a shrine in the Philippines. It was a successful fund raiser, and on July 20, 2003, I attended the dedication in the Philippines on the mountain of Talisay, Lawaan of Cebu.

Schoenstatt covenanters Cynthia Aronson, Gie Best, Juliana Walls, Eppie, Rufino – August 15, 2002.

It was a heavenly feeling when I was inside the shrine. The dedication conducted by Cardinal Vidal, and the afternoon benediction by Bishop Cortes, were two of the most awesome celebrations I ever attended.

Grampas Earl and Nick

During my years at Waterloo High School, Eppie and I came to know Earl Biehle and his wife. Earl was one of the first high school basketball players who made it to state competition. He later served as parade marshal for many Fourth of July parades in Waterloo.

After his wife passed away, Earl visited us almost every weekend at our home in Madison. Our four girls entertained him with their piano playing, singing, and dancing, and he fell in love with them.

Earl always seemed happy when he came to visit and we were pleased to make him part of our extended family. We invited Grandpa Earl, as the girls called him, to several of our summer PAMANA picnics. Shortly before he died in his 92nd year, he was surprised and delighted with a cake that I presented to him at a PAMANA picnic.

When Earl passed away, they found a note on his desk that upon his death I was to be a pallbearer. I felt highly honored.

It wasn't long after Earl's passing that Eppie met an older man on her bus ride to Meriter Hospital. His name was Nick, she learned after chatting with him for three or four minutes.

Grampa Earl with Raechel and Eppie on his 92nd birthday.

It was my custom to pick up Eppie after her shift ended in the afternoon. We fell into the habit of picking up Nick at his apartment at the same time and bringing him to our home for dinner and conversation.

Following Earl's earlier example, Nick also fell in love with our daughters. The girls entertained for him, as they had entertained Earl, and called him Grandpa Nick. He also enjoyed talking with Eppie's parents who were living with us at the time.

On one weekend, we took Nick for a drive around the city. When we returned to our home, he decided to stay for awhile. As usual, he came down from the van with care (he weighed 240 pounds) and started climbing the steps to our front door. There are three steps from the driveway to the first level and three more steps to the main door.

Nick lost his balance on the last step. I was behind him and, as he was about to fall backward, I jumped in front of him and tried to pull him forward, but I lost my balance. To protect him from falling backward, I grabbed his belt and pulled him to one

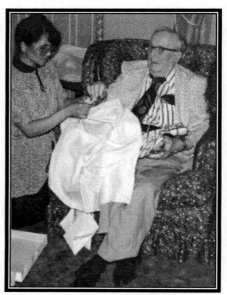

Eppie gives Grampa Nick a new shirt on his birthday.

side. With his weight against my 120 pounds, we landed together at the bottom of the first step, me being under him with my face on the cement. As we untangled ourselves, Nick appeared to be all right, but I was dripping blood from my forehead.

Eppie· instructed me to drive to the hospital emergency room. She was too nervous to drive. Raechel, Eppie and I piled into the car and sped down the road. As I drove, five-year-old Rachael wiped away blood on my head. Eppie sat in the passenger side directing me through the traffic since I was finding it difficult to see clearly. At the hospital, I received seven stitches on my forehead.

Nick felt badly about what happened, but we persuaded him that he had done no wrong, and our friendship remained strong. Over the next two years, we continued to pick him up, drop him off at his apartment, and wash his laundry. When he passed away in a nursing home, we missed him dearly.

Growing with the Girls

Our girls were maturing rapidly, and we were growing just as rapidly in our understanding of their needs. Heidi was very quiet and subtle in her early years. She had only a few hairs sticking up on the middle of her head when she was born, but that changed rapidly and she developed a luxuriant head of hair by the time she was two years old. She was a grandma's girl until she started kindergarten and developed many new friendships. Always a very smart young girl, she would cry if she didn't get a perfect score on her tests or quizzes while she was in grade school.

Heidi enjoyed playing with and feeding Regina (Gina), who was the more quiet of the first two girls. Although Gina seemed to smile constantly, she was quite serious as she pursued the art of maturing into a woman. Her love of schooling lasted throughout her high school years.

Neri was both the most gullible and most playful of our daughters. She had great fun attending school and was not so serious as her two older sisters. She was heavily involved in sports during her school years.

Gina was more prone to accidents. When she was four years old, she was playing with her sisters and cousins while we were visiting in Canada. During the course of play, an earring lock snapped off and went into her ear. We were unable to see the lock and we took Gina to the hospital since she appeared to be in pain. The staff suspected the problem was ear wax. When we returned to Madison, we went to Meriter Hospital

Performing in Spring Green, Wisconsin when Raechel was two years old.

because Gina continued to have ear pain. After a diligent search of the ear canal, the lock was discovered and removed.

When Gina was in third grade, she was run over by a toboggan on the school ground. On a later outing, she ran into a ski being held by another student. She had a number of black and blue facial marks but, fortunately, no other long-term damage.

Left to right: Raechel, Neri, Gina, Heidi, in 1995.

When each of the girls were born, they were in the care of Dr. Yu. They always were glad to have him as their primary physician while they grew up.

In February 1983, when Neri was nine months old, Grandma and Grandpa Avecilla asked to take the three girls to the Philippines for a vacation. Eppie and I would join them four months later. We agreed to the arrangement but soon thereafter had doubts about that decision. Even though the separation was for a short time, we found it difficult to be without our girls. Eppie cried much of the time they were away. Neri was suffering from a cold and having a series of earaches. We called them on the telephone every night as soon as we came home from work. Our phone bill was outrageous.

As soon as school was out in June, we flew to the Philippines. What a reunion we had. Gina, who was a bit over two years old, asked Eppie if she was her real mom.

It was a terrific vacation for the girls and an opportunity for

Grandpa Aguedo and Grandma Caridad, Eppie's parents

them to meet their cousins, aunts, uncles, grandmas, and grandpas in the Philippines for the first time.

Raechel was born three years later. She was an unexpected but most welcome baby who we cherished from the moment of her arrival. Her sisters also loved her. When Eppie was five months pregnant with Raechel, she was struck by a car while crossing the street in a pedestrian walkway. She was rushed to Meriter Hospital's emergency room where she was working as a nurse.

I was teaching at Waterloo High School. My principal, Ted Widerski, came into my classroom and told me of the accident. I left school immediately and drove the thirty-minute trip to Madison in only fifteen minutes that day. Fortunately, Eppie was doing well when I arrived at the hospital, attended by two doctors and two nurses. She was released by the doctor a few hours after I arrived, and I brought her home.

She could hardly sit or stand up to walk into the bathroom that night. I had to help her sit, stand, get out of bed, and lie down again. Our doctor advised Eppie to remain at home while she was in pain. She could consume nothing but oatmeal and red wine without throwing up.

The driver of the vehicle apparently was sentenced to a term in jail for having no insurance, and Eppie received some compensation from our insurance company.

Naturally, we worried about the condition of the baby who was developing inside Eppie. The Simsimans and many other good friends paid us visits now and then to play Mahjongg while we all waited for the wonderful coming event.

When Raechel was born, we were overjoyed and thanked the Lord because she was so healthy and cute. She was the most mysterious and unusual baby of the four girls. When she was eighteen months old, she was playing in the living room in her walking-roller chair. As she glided toward the stairs to the lower level, we realized we had not put the barrier in place. Eppie shouted and I lunged to grab her chair, but I was too late.

Miraculously, Raechel bounced the seven steps to the landing in an upright position. She smiled as we rushed down the stairs, and she continued to smile as we examined every part of her body. There was no damage, and Eppie expressed great thanks to God for sending Raechel's guardian angel to protect her on the way down the stairs. Never again did we forget to put the barrier in place.

Neri, reigning Wisconsin Homecoming Queen, family and friends, perform at the Holiday Folk Fair, 2000.

Grandpa made some rice wine for our dinner when Raechel was two years old. Some of the wine was laced in with the bowl of table rice, as was the custom. Raechel toddled from plate to plate, nibbling at the leftovers, including the table rice, until we placed the plates in the sink. Then she toddled down the hallway. When she didn't reappear a minute or so later, we called out to her and began a quick search. Much to our consternation, we did not find her immediately. We knew she was on the main level of our home, and not in the bathroom, livingroom, or kitchen, but just where she was exploring was unknown.

After what seemed to be a long, long search, but probably was less than a minute, we found her sleeping peacefully in our bedroom closet on top of some blankets. She was none the worse for the experience, which is more than I can say for her parents. We never did determine whether her nibbling the table rice made her sleepy.

At home in Madison, Wisconsin–2003

In the spring of 1978, Eppie was hired by Methodist Hospital (later Meriter Hospital) in Madison. We searched for a house to buy and, fortunately, our realtor, Richard Brockman, showed us a house that was being vacated.

The three-bedroom, ranch-type house at 6017 Rattman Road on the east side of Madison was the first of its kind, built in 1975.

Houses were much less expensive then. A $75,000 house was considered quite expensive. We made an offer and took ownership in May. Moving presented a difficult problem, as any homeowner knows, but my students were kind to help out. I then began to

Gathering in the dining room in 1998; front-Raechel and Gina; rear-Heidi, Neri, Eppie, Rufino

commute daily from Madison to Waterloo, a mild twenty-minute drive. Each work day, I dropped off Eppie at the hospital on the south side and then continued on to Waterloo. At the end of the day, I picked her up on my way home.

Dad moved with us into our new home in 1978. He was alone at home most of the time since both Eppie and I worked during the day. Much of his time was devoted to caring for a large vegetable garden at the rear of our home. He planted string beans, tomatoes, squash, sweet peas, eggplants, and bitter melons.

Additional energy went into cutting our grass once he learned to use the mower. He also raked the leaves in the fall and shoveled the snow during the winter months.

Dad had an opportunity to travel with us when we drove to California to visit his brother, Celedonio, and his family in 1979. We stopped at Las Vegas, Nevada, home of the most concentrated gambling sites in the United States, to visit his nephews Dave and José.

On another trip, we drove to Dearborn, Michigan to visit Dad's sister Antonina, her daughter Ernestina, and Ernestina's family. Dearborn is the suburb of Detroit in which Henry Ford built the Ford Motor Company in 1903. The corporate headquarters still is in a twelve-story building in Dearborn.

Dad traveled with us wherever we went for our summer vacation, including an annual trip to Canada to visit Eppie's brother and their parents.

In the summer of 1992, we returned from an enjoyable Labor Day picnic in Janesville, south of Madison. Eppie and I were talking about the fun we had shared during the day. Our four girls were sleeping in the back of the vehicle. Eppie's mother was sitting behind us.

When we were about fifteen miles north of Janesville on Interstate 90, I glanced at the side mirror and noticed thick, dark smoke coming from the rear of our van.

I quickly stopped on the shoulder of the road. Eppie and her mother brought the girls out of the van while I unlatched the hood from inside the vehicle.

Fire and smoke were coming from the engine. I grabbed my bag and joined my family at the roadside. Cars and trucks stopped behind my van and across the highway. A truck driver brought his fire extinguisher but was too late; the van was completely engulfed by fire before the police and firefighters arrived. Several helpful onlookers offered us a ride to our house. As it happened, the parents of Heidi's classmate drove by and took us home.

Rufino and Gina inspect the remains

On the following day, Eppie and I went to the salvage yard to remove items we had left in the van the day before. The van was completely burned except for a bumper sticker bearing the name "Holy Hill", a well-known Catholic church in Washington County. We had purchased the sticker when the van was blessed during the church's Good Friday celebration in March.

Our insurance company determined that there had been a leak in the gas line and they provided us with funds to purchase another vehicle. We were blessed by God that our family survived the incident without injury to anyone.

Gerry Simsiman

We attended a Miss Pre-Teen Beauty Pageant in Milwaukee over the 1992 Fourth of July weekend. When we returned to Madison on that Sunday afternoon, we called Ruby Simsiman, Gina's godmother, to learn the condition of her husband Gerry, who was suffering with leukemia. Ruby told us that he was in serious condition, but that when he had been told of Gina's success in the competition, he had requested her to visit him at the hospital wearing her gown.

Our family had been close to the Simsimans for many years. Ruby, Gerry and their sons Ruben and Roger belonged to PAMANA and were ardent supporters of the dance troupe.

We drove to St. Mary's Hospital on Monday. Gina wore her gown and crown and brought her trophies and flower bouquet. What a sight she made and what a visit! Gerry was so happy to see his goddaughter. That morning, his face glowed with joy as he hugged Gina and they had their picture taken together.

Later in the day, Ruby called and asked if we would bring Gerry home in our van on Tuesday to spend his final days with his family. We readily agreed, but the hospital staff felt the trip would be more comfortable in an ambulance.

His bed was prepared and he slid under the covers. Almost immediately, their dog Cody jumped onto the bed to be closer to his master. Gerry was extremely weak but he managed to call Cody's name softly, and his pet snuggled close to him, looking searchingly at his master's face. Soon friends of the family arrived. Ruby, Eppie and I stood beside the bed as family and friends arrived to say goodbye to a dear companion.

Gerry passed away peacefully that night while Ruby was singing their favorite song.

The Impact of an Accident

The summer of 1995 whirled in with great happiness and anticipation. I again received a contract to teach introductory Spanish to grades school students as well as to assist teaching martial arts for the second year. It was quite an enjoyable experience since I had studied Judo in the Philippines. It was just like a review for me. The primary instructor was Aaron Warnke, holder of a black sash.

On Sunday, July 16, 1995, Heidi, Gina and I went to church alone since Eppie was working that weekend. Neri and Raechel were spending the weekend with Fred and Nattie Bohl and their daughter Maria. Nattie and Maria were active with us in PAMANA. When we entered St. Albert Church, Sister Rosilda Thiel saw us and, as usual, she gave us a hug. After

Sister Rose and Rufino at St. Albert the Great Church

church services, Sister Rosilda Richel came over from the other side of the church just to give us another big hug.

Since Heidi had her driver's license, I let her drive on the way home. When we came to the intersection of Highway 19 and Portage Road, Heidi let all the incoming cars and trucks pass before attempting to make a left turn across the oncoming lane. The last approaching vehicle was a truck that was flashing its left turn signal. The driver moved toward the center of the median to be in position to make the left turn. Heidi began to move across the median in the secure knowledge that the driver would complete his left turn.

Suddenly, the driver of the truck decided to proceed straight ahead. I yelled "Heidi, he changed his mind," but it was too late. Fortunately, I was sitting in the front passenger seat rather than one of my daughters, and I took the brunt of the massive hit on the right front of our vehicle.

I had a distinct feeling of being lifted up off the highway so I could look down at the scene of a horrible accident. How long I was in that position I don't know. Was a decision being made in heaven whether I would be taken to my eternal home or returned to earth to fulfill a specific mission for God? The vision faded and I heard someone calling me.

"Just hold on, sir," I heard a man say with a tone of urgency. "Help is on the way."

Police squads and fire fighters arrived. Time was blurred as they tried to open the front passenger door with a crowbar. I felt no pain at that time, but I did hear Heidi and Gina moaning. Our rescuers removed us from the car one at a time. I was placed in a stretcher where I must have passed out again. I remember no other details of the traffic scene.

I heard the sound of a siren. Opening my eyes, I realized I was lying in an ambulance that was in motion. I wiped my face with my hand and saw blood on my fingers. Someone was holding my shoulder so I could not sit up.

"Just relax, sir, everything will be all right," the man told me. "Your daughters are all right."

I tried to see through my glasses. They were scratched. I gave up focusing and again slipped into unconsciousness.

Eppie's voice was high pitched, excited, ringing in my ears. She was asking many questions. What happened, where did the accident take place? How did it happen? Who was the other person involved in the accident? Who was driving? Once again I opened my eyes and found myself in an emergency room at Meriter Hospital.

I tried to answer all her questions, but I was feeling too uncomfortable to handle any conversation. A stream of doctors and nurses were taking care of us. One after the other, Heidi, Gina, and I were wheeled into the X-ray room to see if we had broken bones or other damage that would show up on the film plates. Surprisingly, I was not in too much pain yet, but I felt dizzy, and I could move about only a bit.

Miraculously, Heidi and Gina were pronounced free from serious injury, and it appeared that my injuries were minor. Ruby Simsiman and Nattie Bohl arrived with Neri and Raechel while we were being examined. Eppie's cousin Reynudo Dacumos and his son Ronnie also learned of the accident and came to the hospital. We remained at Meriter under observation for four hours, and were released at five in the afternoon, Ruby and Nattie were kind enough to drive us home.

It was a hot day and I was worried about the temperature in the house. We didn't need to add a sweltering home to our misfortunes. We were fortunate in having a neighbor who considerately put our air conditioner in the window of our basement that afternoon.

In the middle of the night, I wakened. Pain was spreading fast throughout my body. I cried out in alarm. Eppie helped me stand and make my way to the bathroom. She gave me two Tylenol tablets and guided me back to bed. Thank God my wife is a nurse, I thought. She knows what to do for me.

We talked through the night about God's plan for us that involved such a horrendous accident. He didn't take any of us so He must have a specific purpose for Heidi, Gina, and me surviving a crash with a heavy truck.

Eppie drove me to see Dr. Priest in the morning. He had been taking care of the family for several years and we had complete trust in his judgment. He prescribed medication for pain and told me to see a chiropractor as soon as possible.

Eppie took off the week from work and stayed with me until we could get into the chiropractor's office the next week. The pain was bearable but I constantly was reminded how fragile we humans beings are and how we should thank God every day for our health.

The chiropractor X-rayed my back and learned that my spinal column no longer was straight. He sent the X-ray to Dr. Priest and began to work on my back. At first, I felt that he was prying my bones apart. The intensity of pain was agonizing as he prodded and pushed my body for six weeks. Prodding was alternated with electrical shocks at the shoulders, neck, and upper arms. The shocks relieved some of the pain but I remained seriously uncomfortable into the fall months.

School began but I was not up to the task of standing in front of my students. I couldn't even sit in front of them for any long period of time. I received permission from the principal to take time off, but I desperately wanted to return. Eppie and the children were the most important part of my life, and teaching was the second most important element. I wanted to be with my students again. After two weeks, I telephoned the school secretary and told her I would return the following Monday.

Monday dawned with the promise of a warm and sunny day. Moving slowly with each movement carefully preplanned, I showered, dressed, and ate a small breakfast. I could tell that all was not well, but it was the best I could expect. I was alive and moving; that was the good news for the day so far.

Getting down our stairs to reach the front door was a task I had accomplished hundreds of times without thinking about how many bones, muscles, ligaments, and muscles were involved in that small assignment. Now I became fully aware of how many small elements of my body were called into play just to take on a flight of stairs. It seemed that not one element was following my instructions willingly.

I simultaneously grimaced with the pain and smiled grimly at Eppie. She tried to look like a professional nurse, but her eyes told me she was in as much sympathetic pain as she held her hands close to steady me if I needed help. Getting into the car was another ordinarily simple task that became a nightmare as every muscle declared its intention of bailing out and going on vacation.

Somehow, in spite of Eppie's objections, I drove her to work and then headed toward the Interstate highway that would take me east to Waterloo. Less than five minutes later, I began to feel dizzy. The feeling intensified until I was compelled to pull over at a phone booth and call the school to cancel my intended arrival. At home, I telephoned Eppie. She didn't seem too surprised; another reminder that wives are a good deal wiser than we men suspect.

Dr. Priest took another look at me later that day and wrote a letter to the school stating that I would have to be excused from teaching until I could visit a neurologist. He recommended that I see

Dr. Craig Dopf

Dr. Mark Simaga, a neurologist. Dr. Simaga, in turn, recommended that I visit with Dr. Craig Dopf, an orthopedic surgeon at Meriter Hospital. Dr. Dopf's notes state that his first meeting with Rufino was on September 21, 1995 at the request of Dr. Simaga. His recorded notes state:

"[Rufino] did have significant pain immediately after the accident and, the following day, was worse than the day of the accident. He had chiropractic manipulation as well as physical therapy without significant benefit. He also had moderate weakness in both of his upper extremities.

"He subsequently went on to have a CAT scan myelogram. He did present to my office at that time with an MRI (magnetic resonance imaging). The purpose of the CAT scan myelogram was to clarify what part of the pathology was bony versus soft tissue in nature. The CAT scan myelogram showed that he had a moderate size disk herneation at C3-4 which was indenting his spinal cord.

"He had a huge C4-5 disk herneation which was right paracentral and grossly deforming his spinal chord. He also had spinal stenosis [construction] of the C5-6 disk (mid-neck

118

behind the Adam's apple) which appeared to be secondary to the disk bulging at that level. Repeat physical examination again revealed significant weaknesses in the upper extremities."

Dr. Dopf explained to me that a disk between each bone of the neck acts as a shock absorber for the bones. The outer part of the disk is tough, leathery-type material; the inner part is a gel like rubber cement. When a disk herniates (protrudes), the outside leathery part tears and permits the inside rubbery part to pop out. This happened at two levels in my situation and I developed tremendous compression on my spinal cord.

Normally, the spinal cord should be a cylinder like a sausage, Dr. Dopf pointed out. He said that my spinal cord in that area looked like someone had shoved his finger into the 'sausage' as hard as he could. It was indented from the disk herneation. During my surgery, he pulled the disk herneation a way from my spinal cord and put little blocks of bone from my pelvis into my neck to fill the gaps that the surgical team created when they removed the disks.

Dr. Doph recalls that "we locked the blocks in place with thin plates and screws. Eventually, the blocks that we inserted melded together and became solid. When you fuse a portion of the spine, as we did, those levels no longer move and that puts more stress on the spine above and below the insertion.

"I had a lengthy discussion with Mr. Licos after his work-up was completed about what the problem was, as well as what his treatment options were, as well as the apparent history of his disorder with and without treatment."

To this day, I remember the myelogram procedure as being neither short nor easy on the patient. I lay flat on my stomach with a rolled-up towel under my chin. A technician injected a dye behind my ear with a five-inch needle.

Rufino's friends at
East Towne Mall enjoying coffee
after their daily exercise.

119

After about ten minutes, I felt excruciating pain at the back of my neck. I begged the technicians to work fast. I'm certain they did their best, but the next thirty minutes were a nightmare of pain against which I was helpless.

I elected to have Dr. Dopf perform disk fusion in my neck before the situation became worse. Eppie agreed. She had known Dr. Dopf for some time and had great trust in his surgical skills, as did I.

Dr. Dopf met with us during the next week and confirmed our suspicions that immediate surgery would be advisable. The date was set for December 8, 1995, the day of the celebration of the Assumption of the Blessed Virgin Mother. I prayed hard for her protection, joined by the family and many friends.

I entered the hospital both scared and worried. Dr. Dopf was patient as he explained the consequences and possible side effects of the surgery. The procedure lasted for eight hours. When I wakened, I was wearing a neck brace and had a blood drainage tube poking out from the left side of my neck. My initial reaction was to thank God and the Blessed Mother for giving me another chance to live.

Eppie became my blessed twenty-four-hour nurse. The assigned nurses complained that they could not do anything for me because Eppie stayed one step ahead of them.

Within hours, I noticed that I was having difficulty talking. Dr. Dopf explained that the nerves associated with speech had been compressed during the operation. It became hard for me to swallow and I developed pneumonia. It required several months before I regained what I considered adequate command of my speaking faculties. During that period, I was unable to teach because I could not project my voice for long periods of time.

East Towne Mall walking friends rest with Rufino in the food court.

Dr. Dopf's post-surgery report in June 1997 notes that I did have a bulging disk at C5-6 prior to my surgery. He elected not to address that level at the time of the surgery to try to keep as many levels as mobile on my neck for as long as possible and, thereby, decrease the stress placed on the adjacent levels. Unfortunately, my C5-6 level did become significantly symptomatic within a relatively short time after my surgery. Dr. Dopf was – and remains – reluctant to proceed with any further treatment with the C5-6 level and currently is contemplating which route he will proceed.

Dr. Doph and our family developed a warm relationship over the months. Eppie had been a nurse on the orthopedic ward and had worked with him previously.

"When Rufino came to see me," he says, "it was as though he accepted me as part of his family. He would bring photographs of his children and newspaper clippings. He's incredibly proud of his girls. I would see newspaper items of his dancing and music. I learned that he is very proud of his culture and his children. He has been a lot more open with me than the average person, and he has shared a lot more about his life than I can anticipate from most patients. I would like to know what Rufino's secret is for happiness. He's incredible."

In the meantime, the auto accident legal questions were settled with great success by Rufino's lawyers, James Gutglass and Sharon Long. Investigation of the accident revealed that the truck driver borrowed the truck without the owner's permission and he carried no vehicle insurance.

Our attorneys were patient, understanding, and helpful lawyers. They were able to negotiate the terms of settlement with the Wisconsin Retirement Department. Before we closed the case, they made sure that I was satisfied with the decision of the court. I will never forget these two wonderful Milwaukee lawyers who made several trips to Madison to help us.

Dr. Geoffrey Priest always was my doctor from 1978 until he received a new assignment at Meriter Hospital. He then transferred me to the care of another great man, Dr. James Giesen, who has been my physician since then. (Dr. Kok Peng Yu was our girls' physician who they loved so much.)

Since I retired early with a disability due to the accident, I spent most of my early morning walking outside when the weather is nice. But as soon as it gets cold and rainy, I walk at East Towne Mall with some retired people. I enjoy walking, talking and having coffee with them.

As the years passed, I recovered from most of my physical problems, except that I never regained the ability to write without my hand shaking, and the consequent handwriting illegibility. Fortunately, neither Heidi nor Gina suffered lasting after affects of the auto accident.

Beginning in 1998, I became a substitute teacher at the De Forest Middle and High School. Returning to education, even on a substitute status, helped me maintain my sanity. All the students, faculty, administrators, and staff, were helpful and wonderful to me.

I also worked as a morning security guard at the Dane County Airport in Madison twice a week since it didn't require much lifting or talking. My initial task was to scan passengers when they went through the metal detectors at the gate. Passengers who were unable to pass through the detectors twice without setting off the alarm, were scanned again with hand-held equipment until the reason for the alarm was discovered. I also worked at the X-ray screening table, examining passenger bags as they went along the conveyor line.

Periodically, Federal Aviation Authority (FAA) agents went through the line carrying guns or other banned equipment to test our capabilities. I caught several officers with guns and one with a hand grenade. One FFA officer tried to get past me with a revolver in his boot.

In the short time of my stay at the airport, due to the heightened security following the September 11, 2001 disaster in New York City, I honestly can say that I had the greatest time. The morning crew was wonderful. Sometime I worked at the Main gate; other days I was assigned to the Commuter Gate.

Wisconsin Governor Thompson welcomes Eppie and Rufino to his mansion in Madison during the Christmas season.

The longer I worked at the airport, the more I got to know some wonderful people like Dick Adrian, Roland Borchers, Rolly Coats, Bill Day, Bob Edwards, Marlene Gray, Lucille Johnson, James Keenan, Donald Lehman, Joyce Liska, James Nelson, Estella Reyes, Roger Steven, Russell Uselmann, Sid Waldorf, and Gerald White.

Among the many administrators at the airport, I developed pleasant friendships with Peter Drahn, Greg Donavan, Charles Peterson, Rod McLean, Stephanie Kirchner, Rachel Peterson, and Sharon Bernhard.

Other friends were John and Steve Morgan, Chuck Wells, Diane Schultz, Jerry Schwenn, Bert Hefty, Mike Ross, and Craig Waldon.

Ching Verosa, Governor Thompson's wife Sue, Eppie, and Rufino at the Governor's summer picnic in Madison.

Three very important people who saw to it that the airport was a safe place to work were Officers Dave Carter, John Kessler, and Todd Huppert. These three officers made the airport more pleasant and safe.

David Hesterly, the airport restaurant manager, always was ready to help employees like me when we were on breaks.

Other helpful friends were Judy Nelson, Doris Brux, and Jean Wescott who worked at the gift shop. These and many others made my stay at the airport most enjoyable.

During this period, I had several opportunities to meet Governor Tommy Thompson as he passed through my inspection station before his airplane trips. Through our friends, Dr. Ray and Ms. Ching Verzosa, who were close to the Governor, Eppie and I were invited to the Governor's mansion several times to attend Christmas parties and summer picnics.

I terminated my employment at the airport shortly after September 11, 2001 when airport duty became more complicated and stressful. Those weeks made me more conscious that money is only one reason to work at a given job. Other important factors include the joy you receive in working, the people you work with, and the location and the time involved in fulfilling your duties..

When I was not at the airport, I continued to choreograph and direct Filipino dances. Dr. Dopf recommended that I continue dancing as the best exercise. He was very supportive during my recuperation from surgery. He told me to increase participation in what I enjoyed doing because that would be the greatest exercise for my body and mind. I owe my good health to his continuing attention. He made me whole again.

Chapter 7: Competition

During 1993, we worked long hours with our daughters to develop a dance program. We called our family group the *Philippine Culture of Madison and the Licos Sisters.*

We were fortunate to be invited by P. Emraida Kiram to open the 1993 Asian Moon Festival in Milwaukee. Over the years, we continued to strengthen our performance through a great deal of rehearsing as well as continually performing for senior citizen organizations, nursing homes, and civic groups. In 1998 we were invited to perform at the sesquicentennial celebration near the Capitol building in Madison.

Heidi was crowned *Miss Philippine Centennial of Madison* at Monona Terrace in the summer of 1998. It happened that a week before our performance, the Equitable Life Insurance Company was looking for someone to feature in their magazine, *The Guide.* Our family was invited to become the topic of a feature

Heidi (Miss Philippine Centennial) in Madison with Mom and Dad – 1998.

article in the September-October 1998 Association's issue.

Neri, was crowned *Homecoming Queen of DeForest High School* in October 1999. In November 1999, she was invited to dance at the Macy's Thanksgiving Day Parade in New York City. These activities contributed to the development of her self-confidence, character, and personality development.

During the following April, Neri competed in the homecoming queen state competition for both Wisconsin and Minnesota contestants that was held in Bloomington, Minnesota. On the Sunday morning before the *Miss Wisconsin Homecoming Queen 2000* was crowned, Eppie and I set out to attend mass. Carefully following the directions given by the hotel receptionist, we soon found ourselves lost. Eventually, we found a Lutheran church on Main Street.

September/October 1998

the guide
Equitable Reserve Association

ERA family enlivens
1998 Wisconsin Folklife Festival

Photos Courtesy of Equitable Life Insurance Company

1998 29TH ANNUAL ERA ART CONTEST
SAMPLING OF FIRST PLACE WINNERS

"FISH IN THE SEA"
Scott Swecke (8) Bloomington, MN

"STILL LIFE"
Leah Adgreson (20) Trail River Falls, MN

"FLOWERS #1"
KJ Cutler (69) Kaukauna, WI

"BIG BLUE"
Gilbert Bulduff (73) Hopkinsville, KY

"FARM IN SPRING"
Marie Mauige (85) Germantown, WI

Although Eppie said it would be all right for us to attend Sunday service a the Lutheran church, I suggested that we drive a little further and, behold, we came to St Peter's Catholic Church. We entered just as mass started. Since Neri's middle name is Corine, after Sister Corine, I prayed to the sister to guide Eppie and me during the coming event, and to provide Neri with strength and courage to endure the competition. Eppie told me later that her prayers were similar to mine.

As we left the church after mass, we noticed a nun in a wheelchair near the door. It appeared as though we were the only ones to see her; exiting churchgoers were passing her by without even glancing in her direction. We approached the nun and greeted her. She responded by nodding but not lifting her head to show us her face.

Neri in New York

Eppie and I looked at each other. Was this an apparition that was appearing to just us? Could it be the spirit of Sister Corine assuring us that she had heard our prayers and that Neri would be all right? It was a spiritually uplifting moment that Eppie and I discussed several times that day.

At the competition site, our table was set outside the main auditorium. We wondered why we were separated from the other contestants and their families. We soon found that we were among the tables of judges and the current homecoming queen.

The competition director approached us during lunch and asked if we had received the necessary tickets to enter the judging auditorium. We thanked her and assured her that we would be entering the auditorium shortly. As we entered the huge room and searched for our assigned seats, we found that we had been placed in the front row.

When the contestants were presented at the beginning of the competition, Eppie and I jointly thought that Neri had little chance to win the crown because the other contestants were very tall and beautiful. Neri was very short but just as beautiful in our estimation, and we didn't lose hope.

During the mid-ceremony break, Heidi asked Eppie if she thought Neri would make the top five selection. She suggested that if Neri was unlikely to win the contest, the family could leave earlier due to the 300-mile trip home. We considered the options and decided to remain.

When the five finalists were announced, DeForest High School was called first. I couldn't resist standing up and applauding. Much to my surprise, everyone in the auditorium except Eppie followed my lead. She had not heard DeForest was called and she was startled when Neri walk toward the front of the stage. She gasped and in a loud voice proclaimed, "Oh, Neri, you are a finalist."

The grandmother of another contestant whispered to her daughter as Neri walked up to the stage, "Do you see that? She walks with such a stately manner."

After the finalists were introduced, they were placed in a private room and called, one by one, to answer a single question: If you had a chance to interview the President of the United States, what would you ask him, and why?

Neri–Miss Wisconsin
Homecoming Queen

The first contestant answered that, if President Bush was elected, she would ask him if he will ask his dad for advice how to run the country since he was a former president.

The second contestant said she would ask how the president could improve the education of today's youths since the youth of today will be leaders of tomorrow.

When Neri was called, she said, "If I had the chance to interview the president, I would ask him how could he prevent or minimize violence in the schools across the country?"

The fourth and fifth contestants also were concerned about the education of the country's young people today.

After each contestant gave her answer, they were recognized individually for the final time by walking along the runway. The master of ceremony then asked the judges for the envelope containing the names of the winners. She called the fourth, third, and second runners up. Surprisingly, Neri was not called.

Neri and escort Nick Clar at PANAMA dinner dance – 2000

Now only two girls remained on stage. Before the emcee announced the first runner up, she mentioned that whoever was crowned would represent the state in the national competition at Disneyland in Anaheim, California in August. She then looked at the sheet of paper she had pulled from the envelope, paused to heighten the effect, and announced the first runner up. Everyone from our group stood up and screamed. The first runner up was not Neri.

"The 2000 Wisconsin Homecoming Queen is Neri Licos from DeForest High School," the mistress of ceremonies called out with a broad smile on her face. That certainly was a highlight of our year and a joyful reward for Neri for all the time she had devoted to preparing for the competition..

*   *   *   *   *

In the first week of August 2000, Eppie, Gina, Raechel, Tom David and I flew to Disneyland to watch Neri's week-long national homecoming queen competition. We stayed at the Disney Hotel, a block from Disneyland. Each day we were able to watch people entering Disneyland from our suite.

In addition to the great view we had from our room, we received wonderful treatment from the hotel staff. When our airplane touched down at LAX Airport, where I had arrived in

1968 after my first trip from the Philippines, we were met by Gale Sherrod who had taught earlier with me in Waterloo.

After Gale left the Waterloo school system, he and his family eventually settled in the Los Angeles suburb of Anaheim where he took up teaching in the local School District.

In our Waterloo days, the Licos and Sherrod families lived in adjacent apartments. Gale's two young sons, Sean and Shane, often would visit us at night and on weekends..

Our stay at Disneyland was memorable. On the second day, I received a telephone call from the lobby that an un-named man was looking for me. When I arrived at the lobby, I was greeted by a young uniformed security officer who I did not recognize. I was genuinely surprised when he smiled, shook my hand and announced that he was Sean Sherrod. We had a wonderful reunion right then in the lobby.

Every morning during our visit, Sean and his assistant escorted us to breakfast at the restaurant inside the hotel. Parents of the other contestants observed us for three consecutive days being escorted by the two security officers. The curiosity of one couple eventually got the best of them and they asked who were we that we had security officers protecting us. I jokingly replied that I was about to become the next governor of Wisconsin. That rumor spread quickly throughout the hotel. Contestants from different states began to greet us with a smile and "Hello, parents of Miss Wisconsin."

Eppie and I were enjoying lunch at the hotel restaurant when Goofey, a Disney characters, stopped at our table. I explained that we were from Wisconsin and our daughter Neri was competing to be named a national homecoming queen. I added that Eppie and I were celebrating our twenty-fifth wedding anniversary.

Goofey called over the other Disney characters in the area. Much to the amusement of the other diners, they danced around the table and sang *Happy Anniversary*. Many of the other diners joined in singing along. That was an unforgettable wedding anniversary gift.

On the night of the national homecoming queen crowning, all the contestants were escorted onto the stage by their dads. I also was selected to be one of the dads to escort contestants whose fathers were unable to attend. Indeed, that was another highlight of our trip. Even though Neri was not one of the top ten winners, we were so proud that she was invited to participate in the competition.

Neri (second row center) represents Wisconsin at the Liberty Bowl, December 2000 in Memphis, TN. Photo courtesy of AXA Liberty Bowl.

In addition to being invited to Disneyland, Neri was one of ten *Miss Homecoming Queen* contestants to receive an invitation to attend the Liberty Bowl football game in Memphis, Tennessee during the last week of December 2000. Before the girls were paraded around the city on a beautifully decorated float, they visited St. Jude Hospital (also known as the Danny Thomas hospital for kids). During the following day, Neri and I attended the game and watched with parental pride as all the contestants were presented on the field during the halftime ceremony.

*   *   *   *   *

In January of 2000, I received a telephone call from Veronica Leighton, publisher and editor-in-chief of *Via Times* magazine in Chicago. She said she had heard about me from our friends Dr. Norman and Olive Aliga, and that I had been nominated for the Chicago's *Filipino-American Hall of Fame* award.

Rufino and Eppie (6th and 7th from left) receive award
as Hall of Fame Model Family on January 5, 2001.

This was a total surprise. Veronica added that the nominating committee did not know in which category I should receive the award: father of the family, education, religion, entertainment, or community.

I thanked her and expressed my honor at being nominated for the prestigious award in any category. The article appeared in the November 2000 issue of *Via Times*.

In the middle of August 2002, I received another telephone call from Veronica asking about our family. She was interested to learn that the Licos family had been performing as a family for quite a time.

Dr. Raymond Verzosa and family receive Hall of Fame Award; Rufino and Eppie are at the left with Veronica Leighton, publisher/editor of Via Times Magazine.

Gina and Raechel with their Kids of America awards - 1990.

Several weeks later, I was informed that we had been nominated to enter the organization's Hall of Fame as a Model Family. Some time later, I received a letter from the selection committee stating that we had been voted *The Model Family for 2000* by a unanimous vote of the committee. That was a dream come true. We always should expect the unexpected because God is the greatest. Our plans may not be His plan, but all of God's plans are the best.

The *Filipino-American Hall of Fame* awardees were invited to attend the induction ceremony at the Holiday Inn near O'Hare International Airport on the night of January 5, 2001. Neri was presented during the ceremony as the reigning Wisconsin Homecoming Queen. Our family was honored to be one of the guest entertainers of the evening and we performed Filipino dances for the attendees.

Sitting at the elevated head table among the Hall of Fame awardees helped me understand the excitement others must feel when they receive prestigious awards.

Raechel in Madison

* * * * *

In 1990, nine-year-old Regina and five-year-old Raechel entered the Kids of America competition that was held in Madison. Raechel was crowned America's Most Beautiful, took first place in talent and was named Miss Glamour. Regina took awards in talent, beauty, and glamour in her age category. Both girls went to national competition that summer in Dallas, Texas.

On our way to Texas, we visited President Lincoln's home in Illinois and the Golden Arch in St. Louis MO. It took us two days to drive the one thousand miles from Madison to Dallas with the four girls, Eppie, Grandpa, Grandma and Aunt Marcelina Preposi.

The entire week of competition was both fun and hectic. One of the joys in these events was to see young contestants compete in talent, casual clothes, glamour, and gowns categories.

In the middle of the Dallas event, the sponsors held an adult talent competition. I joined an adult competition involving contestants from twenty-five other states, unofficially representing Wisconsin. The adults were very talented. Some sang, played the piano, recited monologues, did gymnastics, and danced. I performed a Philippine acrobatic dance called *Pinandanggo* during which I balanced a half-filled glass of soda on my head, forehead, and palms, then crawled on the floor and picked up the glass on my forehead with my knees without spilling a drop. The audience appeared to be captivated with every movement. At the end of the dance, the audience stood, whistled, and yelled.

When all the adult contestants were finished, the master of ceremonies announced that the second runner up was a woman who played the piano quite beautifully. The first runner up was a lady who recited a delightful monologue.

"The champion in the adult talent competition is...," he then said, halting for effect. He repeated the phrase twice to keep the audience in suspense. Finally, he announced, "The recipient of a trophy and a hundred dollar bill is from the State of Wisconsin. Mr. Rufino Licos."

The audience stood and cheered. As I passed the table of the judges, one judge called out in a loud voice: "Prove that you deserve to be champion." He handed me a goblet filled with water. I set the glass on my head and slowly made my way to the stage, making the feat look more difficult than it actually was. Everyone cheered again when I leaned over the stage and returned the glass to the judge without spilling a drop of water.

Stopover in Oklahoma on trip home

That same night, another judge met Neri and me in the hotel hallway. He bowed to Neri and said: "You are such a cute little girl. What is your name?"

"Neri," she replied.

"How old are you?"

"Seven."

"Would you like to do a commercial and possibly become an actress some day?"

Neri smiled and did not answer.

"Mr Licos," the man continued, "my name is Peter Sklar. I'm a talent scout from New York and I am looking for young people to become models, actors, and actresses. "Would you like to bring Neri to my room tomorrow at eight in the morning to try out for a commercial?"

The next morning, Neri and I arrived at Peter's hotel room to find several boys and girls, accompanied by their parents, waiting to see the talent scout.

We were called into the suite almost immediately. I noticed a video camera set in place to record the meeting. Peter was a six-foot-four-inch, good-looking middle-aged Caucasian, and I was concerned that Neri would be intimidated by his presence. However, my being with her possibly calmed her and she acted quite in control of her emotions.

Neri and Rufino sail around New York City in 1990.

Peter handed Neri a piece of paper and asked her to practice read the script for a few minutes. I helped her practice. She then sat on a chair in front of the camera and repeated what was in the script.

"Neri, how would you like to come to New York this summer?" Peter asked after the reading.

Neri just smiled with an innocent look on her face. He turned to me after a moment.

"Mr. Licos, I'll talk to you more about Neri," he added.
I thanked him and we left the room.

The remainder of the week was filled with official and family activities. We attended a July Fourth rodeo celebration and took

Rufino and Neri with Roines Alger at Rockefeller Center

several side trips planned for the contestants' parents. This also was a time to meet with Kids of America managers and crews.

At one point, Rachael was almost removed from the competition because she was affected badly by the extreme outside heat of up to 110 degrees. Her cheeks and eyes became swollen but, thank God, the swelling subsided before a decision had to be made.

On the day the awards were announced, the contestants and parents were well dressed and excited. Regina received first place for her talent, first runner up for Miss Glamour, and top ten in the gown competition.
Rachael took second runner up in Miss Glamour, top ten in talent, first runner up in beauty, and top ten in the overall Kids of America. We brought home thirteen trophies. It was fun and exciting. experience not only for the girls but also for us parents and grandparents.

In August of 1990, Neri was invited by Peter to attend a workshop in New York. Neri was only eight years old and Peter wanted her to fly by herself to New York. Eppie and I were concerned about the safety factor. Peter promised to take good care of Neri and he arranged for one of his staff to meet her at the airport. After a great deal of discussion and individual thinking, we finally decided to allow Neri to fly alone.

When the day came for Neri to leave, we drove to the Dane County Airport ten minutes from our home. The stewardesses promised that they would take the best care of our daughter. They hung a large card with Neri's name on it around her neck. It was difficult for us to let her fly by herself, but because of the assurance of safety everyone gave us, we let her go.

As soon as Neri arrived at Newark Airport in New Jersey, we received a telephone call from her telling us that she had been met by a young lady from Peter's office. I spoke to the lady who told me that everything was all right. We felt greatly relieved. Peter then called me to let me know that Neri had arrived in his place safe and sound.

The ten days that Neri stayed in New York seemed so long. But as soon as she returned to Madison, she told us everything she did on her trip. It was great fun listening about her adventures in New York.

At home in Madison. Front: Rose Avecilla, Rufino, Eppie, Caridad Avecilla; rear: Alex Avecilla Sr., Aguedo Avecilla, and Rey Dacumos

The following summer, Neri's Grandma Caridad accompanied her to New York. While Neri attended the workshop to learn the fundamentals of acting, Grandma stayed in New York's Borough of Queens with Roines Alger, the sister of a friend in Madison. Grandma still talks about her experiences in New York.

Neri and I traveled together during her third and

fourth trip to the Big City because Peter asked me to help his staff take care of the young boys and girls in the workshops. When the workshops were completed, Peter rented a playhouse in Manhattan. Representatives from about twenty agencies came to select young people who they thought might become models or actresses and actors for Broadway musicals. Neri had an agent assigned to her to search for acting jobs. At the time Neri was to fly to New York to audition, I was involved in a serious car accident and that ended Neri's potential acting career.

In the summer of 1992, Gina competed in the *Miss Pre-Teen Beauty Pageant* in Milwaukee. Like all the previous events, this was a hectic but exciting competition. Eppie spent hours, days, and weeks decorating Gina's gown with sequins from top to bottom. Gina took fourth runner up over all, first place in Miss Photogenic, and top five in the four-minute speech.

Eppie and I are happy and proud that as parents we had such wonderful years helping our children grow and prepare for their lives as adults. We truly hope that all those who had any part in the developing the lives of our daughters also have benefitted from the association.

Each daughter has been honored for specific achievements during her school years. Heidi and Regina each received a gold medal at her graduation recognizing high scholastic ranking; Neri and Raechal each received a crown for being a homecoming queen in her senior year.

All four girls traveled together extensively during their childhood. They were featured regularly as performers at the annual Asian Moon Festival, the Wisconsin State Fair, and the Madison Civic Center.

Eppie and I encouraged our daughters to take part in activities that interested them in their younger years. Their choices included beauty pageants, playing the piano, pompon dancing, participating in various sports, performing cultural dances, and other extracurricular activities. They became equally competent as members or captains of sports squads.

All these activities taught them valuable lessons as both leaders and contributing team members. They learned to stand on their own feet as individuals as well as to stand at the head of organizations as dedicated leaders.

There is no doubt that God has guided us to prepare our daughters for their adult vocations and the development of personal codes ethics and morals. We constantly remind ourselves and our children that God's grace and patience are critical to our achieving our goals.

* * * * *

In 1993, Raechel and Regina competed for *America's Cover Miss.* Both won in the state competition and the family drove to Florida for the national event. We enjoyed a visit to Universal Studio and celebrated the July Fourth holiday at Disney World. During the week, the girls received seven trophies.

Neri, Heidi, Gina, Raechel, Eppie, Rey and his son Richard Dacumos on a snowy day in Madison – 1993.

Eppie's cousin, Reynudo Dacumos, returned to Wisconsin with us in 1993 after we participated in the *America's Cover Miss* competition in Florida. Rey recently had arrived from the Philippines with his oldest son Richard.

Aguedo Avecilla, Rey Dacumos, Eppie, Rufino and Rey's son Ronnie in Madison in 1994.

They stayed temporarily with relatives in Florida but later moved to New Jersey near the home of Rey's cousin Rizalino Gaetos. Richard worked part time with his Uncle who had a small construction business. He also worked part time in a number of fast food stores.

Once in Madison, Rey was hired at Wood-

139

man's, a large grocery store in the area. A few months later, Richard flew to Wisconsin and also was hired at Woodman's. The two men stayed with us until we found an apartment for them. Within a few weeks, Rey's second son, Ronnie, arrived from the Philippines to be with his father.

Chapter 8: The Joys of Living

In November of 1981, Delia Mariano telephoned Rufino. A university student, she lived with her family in the Eagle Heights neighborhood of Madison while they were working on advanced degrees at the University of Wisconsin-Madison. Rufino visited their apartment the following weekend.

Delia asked if she and other families could practice their native Filipino dances in the Eagle Heights community building.

"It seemed like a great idea," Rufino thought, "and I agreed to work with them for awhile for the sake of getting them together to break the monotonous daily schedule of working and studying. We started with a few families from Eagle Heights. It wasn't long before more students and residents of Madison began to join us at Sunday afternoon practices."

Dancers began to bring food and drinks for snacks. The longer they practiced the more Rufino enjoyed teaching the dances and getting to know the University students.

Dr. Felipe Manalo's wife Monette became Rufino's primary dancing partner at gatherings. Dr. Manalo became well known to all groups due to his beautiful tenor voice. He sang Tagalog Kundiman, love and serenades at gatherings. Their three beautiful daughters, Anna, Isabel, and Kristina, became dancers with both Sampaguita and PAMANA dance troupes

Gerry and Ruby Simsiman also contributed considerable time to running the

Monette and Rufino
perform the Lerion Dance

Gerry and Ruby Simsiman

organization. Ms. Pat Chapagain, then a student and Eagle Heights resident, was very much involved in practices. She was a great dancer herself.

Filipino resident and student organizations had existed for several years along the Milwaukee-Madison corridor. Saturnino Doctor, the acting president, Francisco Piñalba and Rufino were PHIL-AM (Philippine American Association) vice-presidents. Francisco represented the university students and Rufino represented the Madison residents. Agnes Cammer also was very much involved in the organization.

Rufino remembers the chain of events.

Soon the group became increasingly ambitious. They asked if Eppie and I could help them form a Filipino dance troupe since children, young teenagers, and adults were becoming increasingly interested.

The Sampaguita Dance Troupe was formed. The sampaguita is the national flower of the Philippines. Over time, members became increasingly serious about the group's purposes and, eventually, scheduled a show for May 2, 1982. They organized a event planning committee, and Rufino requested Pat and another dancer to help at practices. Action committees were formed and assignments were accepted by members.

Costumes for the dances, narration for the presentation, props, and music needs were addressed. I was appointed choreographer and director for the Sampaguita Dance Troupe of Madison. In turn, I asked Pat to take on the responsibilities of the assistant director. We practiced every Sunday afternoon at the Eagle Heights community building from one until five. The cooperation of everyone was tremendous.

One "happy" problem existed. Eppie was expecting her third child the week before the show. Everyone prayed for an early (or much later) delivery. Fortunately, our third daughter was born on April 27, a week before the scheduled performance. We were relieved and the cast and crew were doubly happy.

Rufino performs the Singkil Dance
with friends in Madison

We named the baby Neri in honor of Saint Philip Neri, my patron saint when I was in high school. We selected Corine as her middle name in honor of Sister Corine with whom we worked at St. Albert the Great parish in Sun Prairie, which we had joined in 1978. Sister Corine was delighted that our daughter was named after her.

The show on May 2nd was well attended and well applauded. We realized all our expectations. Cynthia Bautita narrated and presented an excellent history of the Philippines. The dances from the Luzon, Visaya, and Mindanao regions were elegant and graceful, highlighted by colorful costumes from rural areas, as well as Spanish and Muslim influences.

The stage background with slide projections of different views and sceneries was beyond description. When the final curtain came down, Cynthia thanked the audience for its presence and support. Then she called my name.

Neri, Gina, and Raechel perform the Igorot Courtship Dance – 2002

"Ladies and gentlemen, I have great pleasure presenting to you our show's director and choreographer, Mr. Rufino Licos." There was applause from the audience as I came out. I thanked them for their appreciation and support. I then called the full ensemble of the Sampaguita dance troupe onto the stage and the audience stood as they applauded.

Finally, I asked Delia Mariano to step forward, introducing her as the innovator of the dance troupe.

From that single, successful show, the Sampaguita Dance Troupe became well known in the Madison area. Soon it was invited to join the annual International Festival at the Madison Civic Center with a thirty-minute presentation. The troupe also received affiliation with the University students, allowing them to use University facilities for practices and shows.

We weren't without our distractions amidst the applause, however. Pat Chapagane married Saturnino Doctor Jr. The newlyweds then moved to Fresno, California and the troupe lost two valued members. We were fortunate to find another member of the dance troupe to help teach certain dances.

While Sunday practices the University's Union South were progressing well, one dance required new costumes. Eppie's mother, Caridad Avecilla, who had sewn the previous costumes, was fully occupied taking care of the Licos' three daughters, and unable to devote the needed attention to making the troupe's costumes. A talented lady in the troupe offered her skills to sew the sixty-five-dollar costumes.

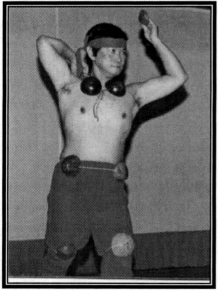

Rufino dancing the Maglalatik

As the day of the performance came closer, practices became increasingly more serious. A member who was helping dancers practice the *Igorot* and *La Jota Moncadeña* dances suggested that a mirror be brought to rehearsal so those who wished to do so could practice their smiles. That was a great help.

The performance at the Civic Center was a huge success. Following that event, the troupe was asked to perform regularly at the Civic Center. We also continue to receive invitations to perform at senior centers, churches, nursing homes, and local festivals.

As performance schedules became increasingly active, many troupe members strained to take care of homes, families, jobs, and church responsibilities. Our family was no exception. Eppie was busy at Meriter Hospital, I continued my daily teaching schedule at Waterloo High School, and our in-laws took care of our three girls.

In 1984, the troupe decided to change its name. A contest was arranged to select a "meaningful, original, and striking" title. Many good suggestions were submitted, and the members eventually selected the name 'PAMANA', submitted by Pat Chapagane. Pamana means heritage in the Filipino language.

Applying the individual letters as an acronym, the troupe now is the *Philippine American Association of Madison and Neighboring Areas*, and serves as an organization of local residents and University students who have strong ties to The Philippines and its people.

The group decided to celebrate Philippine Independence Day in the month of June, beginning in 1986. The celebration was moved to July in 1987, due to difficulty in reserving a place to enjoy the accompanying dinner dance.

PANAMA song composed by Olivia Aliga in 1984

Our Maturing Family

At the same time the dance troupe was maturing, so were Heidi, Gina, Neri, Raechel, and their parents. I continued to teach at Waterloo High School, instruct Filipinos in the art of native Filipino dances, and perform at numerous organizations. Eppie became a staff nurse at Meriter Hospital in 1978 and still managed to find time to perform with me.

The girls became more proficient in singing and dancing. Heidi studied both the piano and rondalla. a fourteen-string Filipino instrument. She entered the Kids of America competition, winning third place as she played a Filipino song, *O Naraniag a Bulan,* on the rondalla. This was quite an accomplishment for a girl who had been very shy as she grew up.

We are equally proud of each daughter. They have used their excellent upbringing and scholastic accomplishments to place themselves in roles as leaders wherever they are. They always have been well mannered. Each Sunday, as they grew up, they each sat quietly and attentively with us in the front pew at St. Albert the Great Church. There was never a time that they misbehaved in church, in a shopping mall, or at a restaurant.

When friends asked us why our girls were so well behaved, respectful, and polite, we replied that they were raised to respect their elders, beginning with calling our friends tito (uncle), tita (aunt), grandma, grandpa, *manang* (older sister) and *manong* (older brother). Our neighbors and acquaintances were to be addressed as Mister and Missus.

We were invited to perform near Spring Green in the summer of 1987. For the occasion, we taught Heidi, Gina, and Neri to perform a Hawaiian dance to the music of *Pearly Shells.* Shortly before the second performance, two-year-old Raechel decided she wanted to dance with her older sisters. Eppie found an extra lei and grass skirt and took her onto the stage. Her appearance brought the audience to their feet with applause and broad smiles.

Xavier Puzon, Neri, and Raechel enjoy the 2000 Sun Prarie, Wisconsin Corn Festival Parade

We found ourselves in tears as we watched our four children dance together for the first time. From that occasion forward, the girls danced as a team.

The troupe performed throughout Wisconsin and Illinois as far as Onalaska on the Mississippi River to Chicago on Lake Michigan. In addition to it's annual performance in Madison, the dancers also performed periodically at the Wisconsin State Fair in Milwaukee and on The University of Wisconsin's Oshkosh campus in April 1987 during the campus multicultural month.

When our daughters were in middle and high school, we began to perform as a family. We are known variously as *The Philippine Culture of Madison* and *The Licos Sisters*. In 1993. We were the first family act to perform at the Asian Festival in Milwaukee. We also performed at the Ethnic Triangle Festival in Madison and the Corn Festival in neighboring Sun Prairie. Most of our performances were twenty to forty minutes long.

I'm proud to note that although the girls maintained a heavy dancing schedule, they kept up with their studies and also were active in sports. In the middle school, they all played volleyball.

Ruby Simsiman

Ruby was a research specialist at the McArde Laboratories for Cancer Research, University of Wisconsin-Madison, in 1973. Her husband Gerry was a graduate student pursuing his Ph.D. in water chemistry and environmental studies at the University. He joined the faculty that year.

The Simsimans were at a picnic in Vilas Park with other Filipino families when Ruby observed Rufino taking a leisurely walk in the area. She and Gerry struck up a conversation and years of good conversations and friendship commenced.

During successive meetings and parties, Rufino became close to the Filipino community in Madison and mutual friendships were formed. Ruby explains:

"Since we are away from our biological families who live in the Philippines, we Filipinos who live in the United States seek comfort with each other. Thus, we form a cultural family. After a long week of work, we look forward to seeing each other, whether it be at a picnic or home parties. These events have become a tradition that we maintain today. They are our best way of keeping in touch.

Ruby Simsiman

Ruby recalls that after the group came to know Rufino for some time, various members tried to match him with eligible bachelorettes in the group.

"But what we didn't know was that he was traveling frequently to Winnipeg in Canada to see his lady love, Eppie Avecilla. We finally met Eppie after the wedding when she moved to Wisconsin."

"If you don't know Rufino from the heart, there are times that you shy away from him because he's so outspoken. Even so, he's a man of good heart and very understanding. He always goes out of his way to be cheerful and giving, always wanting to share joyful occasions, and always ready to lend a helping hand to those who need it.

"Eppie is very quiet and reserved. Rarely do we hear her complain, even if Rufino forgets to pick her up at the end of her work shift. She knows, as we all do, that he tends to spread himself too thin as he accommodates and helps others, even to the extent of sacrificing his own schedule.

"I have reminded Rufino several times that there are nice ways to tell people he can't take on their particular project because he has too much else to accomplish. He always tries to accommodate others while forgetting his own needs, particularly the need to rest. He has to learn how to say *no* sometimes."

Ruby recalls that all of Rufino's willingness to help and be an active part of the community was exemplified in February 1982 during the formation of the Sampaquita Dance Troupe of Madison.

"Members of the dance group comprised a cultural group that contributed its talents in Filipino folk dancing. Since all the members were hard-working job holders and students, we tried to fit our practices into our busy schedules. Nights became days for us as we practiced until the wee hours, often until two in the morning.

"With our busy schedules and the hard work ahead of all of us, we almost gave up the whole idea of a dance troupe, but Rufino was determined to push on with the project. With his encouragement, coupled with everyone's determination, we were able to reach our goal. Four months of hard work for all of us became a dream fulfilled when we painstakingly and cheerfully made our first remarkable presentation in May 1982. We were the Sampaquita Dance Troupe of Madison after all with Rufino as our director."

Rufino and Eppie are accommodating to friends and strangers alike, Ruby asserts.

"They always open their hearts as well as their home to everyone. Need a social hall and can't find one, ask Rufino. He'll offer his home. Rufino and Eppie always will be at everybody's beck and call, regardless of the time of day or the weather conditions.

"Both Rufino and Eppie are deeply religious and an inspiration for us all. They remained with me and my family constantly during my husband's final days. They were there for us when we needed them most, offering their unconditional love and care."

Ruby believes she has formed and maintained a solid relationship with the Licos family through the years that includes the four daughters. She is Gina's baptismal god-mother. The girls listen when she talks, she says, and they do what she asks of them. They all treasure the familial relation-ship.

"I keep in touch with the family, especially the chil-dren. I'm proud to say that I have found my family in Madison among all my friends. When I visit the Phil-ippines, I can say I'm with my biological family, but when I'm in Madison, our friends are our family. Thus, I can proudly hold dear the saying: Faithful friends are life's best treasure."

Dr. Dennis Mariano

Dennis Mariano holds a special relationship with Rufino. A graduate of the University of the Philippines, he is a practicing veterinarian, specializing in livestock medicine. Dennis is retained as a consultant by farmers, most of whom have business interests in Manila. In 2002, he opened a clinic in Makati, Manila's major business district. Thirty percent of the seven hundred twenty million people living in the Philippines live in the Greater Manila district.

The veterinary industry is developing rapidly as Filipinos change their attitude about small animals, Dennis explains. Whereas dogs and cats once required no special attention, human masters today are learning to think of their pets as family members who require much the same attention as do humans.

"Mom and Dad were friends with *Tito* (uncle) Rufino. I was seven years old when we first visited the United States for a three-year stay. I remember picnics around Madison and an international food festival where we showcased our Filipino products. I also remember the adults practicing many nights for a dance troupe performance. Mom and Dad were involved in the troupe. My brother and sister and I would be left at home so our parents could go dancing. We also went to Christmas parties with other Filipinos."

Agnes Gutierrez Cammer

Agnes Cammer's husband passed away in September 1979. One of her employees, Conchita, who became a dear friend, asked if she might invite members of the Filipino community to the funeral.

Agnes replied that she knew only one Filipino in Wisconsin other than Conchita. Any Filipino was welcome to attend the funeral She remembers the result of that invitation.

Agnes Cammer

"There are about five hundred Filipino families in the Madison area. Much to my surprise, a sizeable number came to the visitation and funeral. Rufino was one of them. When it was time to prepare for the prayers that are said nine days after the funeral, Conchita asked if we were going to have a Filipino prayer meeting.

"I suggested that she organize the meeting. The Filipino group came to our house on Saturday, bringing several pots of Philippine cuisine. Rufino, Ruby Simsiman, and Conchita and her husband were the big cooks. We fed two or three dozen Filipinos and other guests in the house. It happened to be the day of a college football game, and people who went to watch the Badgers play for the University of Wisconsin in Madison came to the house after the game."

From then on, whenever a significant event took place in the Filipino community, Rufino invited Agnes to attend. She lived only two miles away and Rufino always offered to drive her to the event. Agnes eventually became one of the founders of PAMANA.

Year after year, Agnes was invited to the Licos home whenever Rufino and Eppie hosted an event. Her grandchildren attended later events.

"In 1989, when my granddaughter Samantha was born, Rufino and Eppie became her godparents and our relationship became one of family as well as friendship. Eppie's parents took care of Samantha occasionally.

"When I invited Rufino to a meeting of the Wisconsin Organization for Asian Americans because we were going to show the video *The Color of Fear*, he met many of my good friends. Even today, he joins me when I host a new group with whom I want him to share experiences.

"Rufino always is willing to help others, and I wonder if he occasionally is overwhelmed by his commitments. For instance, during a single day recently, Rufino took a woman shopping, then he went to pick up one of his children. After he dropped her off at home, he picked me up to go to the Rizal-MacArthur Memorial Foundation meeting in Milwaukee.

"We had dinner at the New China Buffet in West Allis (a western suburb of Milwaukee), after which he patiently attended my meeting. He said he was so glad he was invited. Then he drove us back to Madison, dropped me off at my home and returned to his family."

"Rufino is very community oriented and he gives of himself with deep commitments to many people and projects. I suspect that some people take advantage of his willing nature. I'm certain he notices when he's being put upon, but he accepts gracefully everyone who comes to him for help. No matter how much time and energy Rufino puts into projects to help others, some people will say negative things about him. Fortunately for us, he accepts most of the barbs without comment as continues to lead the community.

"Rufino is emotional, passionate, and spiritual. That probably dates to his pre-priesthood days in Vigan, Ilocos Sur. Today he still is heavily involved with his church and the Schoenstatt Sisters. When someone passes away in the community, he usually is invited to lead the prayers."

Beginning in 1982, Agnes says, Rufino put countless hours into developing the skills of the men and women in the Madison dance troupe. At one point, he invited all interested people to practice — Filipinos and others. If someone had the heart and interest to learn to dance, they became part of the troupe. Aspiring dancers came to practice every week from many out-of-town locations.

Rufino has a good sense of humor, Agnes confirms, but he is not one for practical jokes.

"He becomes upset when he sees others being hurt through unfair treatment. His true friends likewise become annoyed when they see Rufino help others who then turn around and hurt him."

Agnes suggests that writing a book about his life allows Rufino to prepare a legacy for his family as well as for many adults and children in the Philippines.

"Rufino will be remembered for offering himself and his resources to help others. I hope he will continue to focus on creating awareness and understanding among our communities here to recognize the needs of our people in the Philippines and to make positive contributions in improving the Filipino quality of life."

Princess Emraida Kiram

Princess Emraida Kiram is a Muslim princess of Tausug and Maranao ancestries, from Mindanao, Philippines. The daughter of Sultan Kiram, she maintains residences in Wisconsin and Marawi City, Lanao del Norte, and Kidapawan, North Cotabato.

Educated in the Philippines, London, and Madrid, she was the first Miss Philippines candidate to enter the Miss World Competition.

"When the Asian Moon Festival was struggling to become recognized in the early 1990s, we found it difficult to attract enough Filipino performers to take part in the event. Desperate to achieve greater representation, I called Rufino for assistance.

"Without hesitation, he agreed to transport his family and several friends to Milwaukee ninety miles away, driving back to Madison after each night's performance and returning for more performances the following day over a three-day run. They gave the Festival their undivided attention not just once, but over a period of several years.

"The Madison-based performers did all this without compensation and, as I now recall with a good deal of embarrassment, without even an offer to reimburse them for gas money."

Rufino's wife, Eppie, and their four gorgeous daughters — Heidi, Gina, Neri, and Raechel — each are as committed as Rufino, Emraida says.

"I have not seen a family so dedicated and so admired. Perhaps there are more affluent Filipinos, perhaps there are more famous Filipinos, but none can equal the role models they are to others. We can be proud to be their friends, and we can take pride in their achievements for they embody all our dreams and aspirations as individuals and as a family."

Developing a Filipino presence in the community became much easier when Rufino became involved, Emraida maintains, noting that everything centers around Rufino. He can motivate people wherever he goes.

"I met Rufino and his family at a dinner dance in Madison. He was the cultural director of the Filipino dance troupe at that time. We became close friends almost immediately. I sensed then that the family centers around Rufino because of his personality. He is very warm, even if you're meeting him for the first time. He's always smiling and very open. He immediately wants to know your roots in the Philippines. Then he invites you to Madison where you may stay with his family. Eppie has the same personality but is more quiet in her public exposure, allowing Rufino to be the center of attraction."

The Asian Moon Festival was founded in Milwaukee in 1993. Emraida became involved with the Festival when it was in its infancy.

"Each of us who represented an ethnic group wanted to enhance our ethnic participation at the Festival. The Filipino leadership in Milwaukee at the time felt that Filipinos already were well known, that we had *arrived*, and that we had made a reputation for ourselves. So what was in the Festival for us?

"I wasn't looking at it that way. The Wisconsin Organization for Asian Americans (WOAA) was founded in Madison. Milwaukee became a chapter around 1991. When the WOAA was organized, there were three Filipino members: Agnes Cammer, Leticia Smith, and I. The Asian Moon Festival was not part of the original structure; it became a project of WOAA-Milwaukee."

"The idea of an Asian festival did not come easily. Many Asian groups, the Chinese and the Japanese groups, were first approached. They felt they could not sustain an annual festival by the themselves, so they initiated meetings with other Asian communities.

"The steering committee then heard of WOAA- Madison and approached them to determine whether a WOAA-Milwaukee chapter was feasible."

A group called the March Against Family Violence (MAFV) scheduled an event in Milwaukee for the same weekend in 1993 as the Asian Moon Festival. They asked WOAA to join in the march. Emraida asked Rufino if the Licos family would perform at the stops as the march moved throughout the city. He agreed, and the family was well received by the public.

Rufino became involved in PAMANA in 1980 when the organization was known as PHIL-AM, and accepted the presidency of PAMANA for the 2001-2002 term.

"Rufino and Eppie are always ready to help others. I recall when I invited three out-of-town Catholic priests to join me at the Wisconsin Dells, a noted recreation site sixty miles north of Madison. The priests were unable to find hotel rooms at the Dells. Rufino and Eppie somehow learned of the predicament and invited everyone to spend the night at their home.

"I had flu and went to bed almost as soon as we arrived at the Licos' home. The priests stayed up most of the night with Rufino and Eppie. In the morning, I learned that Rufino had been a seminarian in the Philippines, and the four men had found a great deal to discuss.

"I've never seen Rufino at any time when he hasn't been outgoing and welcoming of others. He's both a good follower and a good leader. I've never seen him angry or even upset. It doesn't seem to be in his philosophy or nature. He is recognized wherever he goes. I remember walking with him in a mall in Madison. Half the people there knew him."

"Rufino has great love for his children and he is very proud of his wife Eppie who is very successful in her nursing profession. Their children are beautiful, talented, and there is no rivalry among them. Many people become successful within their own professions or family, but they don't share with others in the community as do the Licos family members.

"Rufino will be remembered because of the cultural activities he has founded and in which he has participated. He also will be remembered because he is so well loved. You have never seen anyone with such a big heart. He excludes no one."

Emraida spearheaded the development of the Wisconsin Chapter of the Filipino American National Historical Society (FANHS) in 2002. When FANHS was looking for a conference site, she made a bid to have it in Wisconsin, contingent upon the willingness of St. Norbert College to host the group.

"I was thinking of St. Norbert's College in De Pere, Wisconsin which has a Philippine Studies program and is the only college in the continental United States that has such a program. I wanted Filipinos in Wisconsin and the Midwest to learn more about Filipino events taking place around the country.

"The FANHS search committee hesitated to come to Wisconsin because we had not formed a chapter and De Pere seemed far away from everything. I told them that the college was ten minutes from Green Bay and the neighboring Oneida with its famous casino."

FANHS Midwest did hold a highly successful conference in Wisconsin. During that weekend, Emraida organized the

FANHS Wisconsin chapter and Rufino became a founding member. The local unit is unusual in that it has no officers. A roundtable of members discusses Society matters and selects a chair for each event with which it becomes involved. Thus, all members take turns in leadership roles, working closely with others as they develop their capabilities.

Rufino called Emraida at 10:30 one evening. He seldom called at night, so she instantly waited to hear bad news. But that night was different.

"I had to call you," he said, "because we have a house guest from Canada. He was looking over the photographs of our daughters and he saw your picture. He said he knew you in the Philippines."

Rufino then turned over the telephone to Danny Cabatan, an acquaintance from Emraida's university days. Danny's cousin was her classmate and his parents picked up Emraida each day on their way to school. When the cousin tragically passed away in his senior year, Emraida brought the classmates and parents together at the University and took care of the funeral arrangements. She then arranged with the University president to have Danny's cousin awarded an honorary diploma.

Emraida and Agnes Cammer return to the Philippines with a medical mission every two years on behalf of the Rizal-MacArthur Foundation where both serve as Trustees. The Foundation was created in Milwaukee in 1966 to collect and ship medical supplies and equipment for medical facilities in the Philippines.

[Jose Rizal (1861-1891) is a national hero. A crusader against the tyrannies of Franciscan, Augustinian, and Dominican friars who held the country in political and economic paralysis, he was executed by a Spanish firing squad prior to Philippine independence from Spain in 1898. American General Douglas MacArthur (1880-1964) is considered the liberator of the Philippines from Japanese oppression toward the end of World War II.]

In 2002, Emraida and Agnes' missionary work took them to Bacnotan La Union, the home town of Rufino's dad. Eppie called ahead and her mother welcomed the ladies and spent an afternoon together.

"We're pleased that Rufino's life achievements will be chronicled in a book that will be circulated in Filipino communities around the world. Many Filipinos who grow up in highly politicized communities believe that a primary goal should be to become a senator or governor of their state. But that's not what life is about. Life is the ability to achieve one's potential as a person and then reach out to many people who honor you or appreciate what you've done. Rufino and Eppie are models of this capability."

Norma and Dorothy Clemente

Norma and Dorothy live in Oak Creek, Wisconsin, a southern suburb of the City of Milwaukee, with a population of 27,000 people. Norma was a sponsor at Rufino and Eppie's wedding.

Dorothy is Norma's daughter and godmother to Heidi. Norma speaks highly of the Licos family.

"Rufino is a very caring person, very religious. You can depend upon him when he is needed in any way. He is always available to help, and he is like a son to me.

"I don't know anyone who does not like Rufino. However, I do believe some people envy him because he has so many talents. If someone can get along with everyone in a community and can handle many projects at one time, others may criticize that person.

Norma and Dorothy Clemente -

"The Licos home is like a train station. When a group of Filipinos came to Wisconsin in 2002 to perform dances, Rufino and Eppie insisted that the Licos family host them all.

"I don't know how many there were. The children were not well off and they were here to raise money, clothes, and the consciousness of their existence to Filipinos in Wisconsin. The Licos' gave them clothes and other items to take back home."

When Rufino joined the dance troupe and drove to the Milwaukee rehearsals, the Clemente's came to know him better.

"He was an active member of the original Filipino dance troupe that performed many times for nursing homes, schools, and the community. Everyone wanted to be Rufino's dancing partner," Norma says.

The Clementes agree that some of Rufino's important values include his religious beliefs, love for his family, and absolute honesty.

"He is one person who you can really trust," Dorothy emphasizes. "Most of what he does is out of the goodness of his heart. There are no pretensions. On the outside, Rufino never appears to be angry. He does become frustrated from time to time over people who talk badly of him. He is a model father and Eppie is a model mother. His girls love and respect them because of how they have been brought up."

Dorothy recalls that when she was studying at the University of Wisconsin in Madison, Eppie and Rufino opened their home to her on weekends.

"I would drive to Madison for classes on Saturday morning and return to Milwaukee at night. Rufino knew I was tired and he insisted that I rest until Sunday. I would waken and find him up and cooking breakfast with a cheerful smile. 'You're like a sister to me,' he insisted, 'and I would rather have you rested before you drive home.'"

Isabel Maria Piana

Isabel Maria Piana retired in 2003 as a kindergarten teacher and unit leader at Thoreau Elementary School in Milwaukee. She is the comadre (godmother) to Heidi.

> "I graduated from college in 1969, and it was in December of that year when I met members of the original Filipino dancers who became part of the dance troupe during the following year. It was in the summer of 1970 when we started the group in Milwaukee. We were getting together to dance and just have fun socializing. We usually met on Friday nights. Our first meetings were at St. Michael's Hospital on Villard Avenue. They had intern quarters that were perfect for meetings and dances."

The dance director was Ms. Santos and Rufino was one of the dancers. Many of the participants learned to dance at the St. Michael's sessions. After their practices, they occasionally visited night clubs and continued dancing to the delight of those around them.

The group's primary purpose was to learn Filipino folk dances and perform in public to spread the Filipino culture. With that goal in mind, they named their group *Silahis*, which means rays of the sun.

> "Our idea was to spread sunshine among people for whom we were performing."

Isabel was born and raised in Milwaukee at a time when the Filipino community consisted of about twenty-five families.

> "Dad was a native Filipino, born in La Union Province, as was Rufino; Mother was Mexican-American,

born in Texas. Dad came to America when he was nineteen years old. I believe that he and Rufino became such good friends partly because they both were born and raised in La Union Province.

"When Dad came to America, there were not many Filipino women here. Consequently, Filipino men married women of other nationalities. Dad met Mom in Milwaukee. Mother's aunt threw a party to which Dad was invited from Chicago. They started to date, with Dad traveling the ninety miles to and from Chicago for each date. After they married, they settled in Chicago."

Many Filipinos who have intermarried are not aware that Filipino communities exist to keep ties with the "old" country, Isabel points out. There are substantial Filipino populations in Los Angeles, Philadelphia, San Francisco, Chicago, and New York City. The Milwaukee-Madison community is small compared with the populations on the east and west coasts.

"I believe that many Filipinos would welcome marriage within their native population but a loving, kind and supportive spouse is more important."

Isabel's greatest memory of Rufino is with a big smile and great enthusiasm about dancing. He always seemed to be in motion, teaching and leading others on the dance floor.

"Our mutual profession of education helped us develop a strong bond. We constantly talked about our programs and students. Rufino was very friendly and open, and a great dancer. When you danced with him, even if you had two left feet, you felt like you were Ginger Rogers dancing with Fred Astaire.

"Rufino has the ability to bring out the best in people, particularly if they're just beginning to dance. He is very respected in Wisconsin as an educator, dancer, and family man. He was honored as a Wisconsin Outstanding Young Educator in 1973-74, and he was presented with a plaque as a member of the 2000-2001 Model Family Hall of Fame in Chicago."

Isabel's friends held many picnics at Hawthorne Glen on the border of Milwaukee and Wauwatosa. Her godparents, Peter and Mary Adriano, were well-known in the community as Uncle Pete and Aunt Mary. New Filipino families often met at their house, and that's how Isabel was introduced to a number of couples. The dance group sprang from those meetings.

Isabel had learned only one dance, and that was when she was a college freshman. An American girl of German heritage taught her how to dance the *tinikling,* her first Filipino dance. She had learned it as a Girl Scout at Mount Mary College.

During her student years at Mount Mary, she occasionally modeled with a group from Marquette University that held fund raisers for various causes. Isabel attended the functions dressed in native Filipino clothes. Rufino joined a succeeding troupe, the Silahis Dancers, that formed in the late 1960s.

"Rufino was living in Waterloo in the 1970s, and he either had not met, or he was engaged to Eppie. He would travel from Waterloo to Milwaukee, a round trip distance of 125 miles. I recall doing a show for the Waterloo High School. There were so many of us that we hired a bus to take us up to the school. Rufino cooked for us. My Jewish girlfriend and her boyfriend followed us in their car and thoroughly enjoyed the Filipino dishes Rufino prepared.

"I still love to dance and I wish I had more time to learn new dances. My favorite is dancing the umbrella lady in the Singkil courtship dance from the Muslim sector of the south Philippines. There is a dance troupe today in Milwaukee but it's not quite so active as it was years ago. People have moved on and are not able to participate as much.

"We have a young group coming up, but it's not quite the same for me as in the 'good old days'. Most of us were single or newly married and dancing was part of the recreation in those days, along with picnics. However, after thirty-plus years, the Silahis Dancers continue to entertain.

"Rufino started another group when he moved to Madison and, because he had family involvement, he probably danced more than the rest of us. These days, dancers from Madison and Milwaukee continue to join forces occasionally for special occasions like the Holiday Folk Fair."

Because Isabel is Heidi's godmother, she maintains a special relationship with the Licos family. She doesn't see her goddaughter as much as she would like, but Rufino and Eppie remain close.

"Their house always is very open, and my mother and I visit when we're in the area Our interest in education, dance, and music, plus the connection with the children has helped to keep us together all these years. The family comes first, and I'm fortunate to be considered part of the family.

"Throughout the Filipino community in Wisconsin, most families are close. We may not see each other often, but when we do start talking, it's like we never were apart. We feel that we can confide in others if we need to do so, yet there is a sense of privacy accorded to each person. If you want to talk, that's fine. If you just need a hug, that's fine, also. If you don't want to talk, that's still fine. There's always a presence that you feel."

Rufino is upbeat most of the time, Isabel confirms. He is sad when he is at a funeral of a good friend, and he also is sad when his children don't meet his expectations at a particular time – even though he still loves them dearly. He takes enthusiastic pride in each of his children and their accomplishments.

"Whenever he talks of them, you can sense his immense pride. The girls have a great love among themselves, and that has to come from the parents. Even though the children are grown now, the family continues to enjoy many activities together.

"Rufino never seems to be embarrassed. He often is a leader but never by fiat. He just gets projects going and people join in to help him. You're not aware that he's leading the project."

Isabel believes Rufino and Eppie have a very loving and supportive relationship.

"They live for each other and their children. Their interests are similar. They consider themselves equal partners without one dominating the other. The dance troupe probably would not have continued for such a long time without Eppie's support. She was responsible for washing, ironing, and beading the costumes, and her other quiet, behind-the-scenes work for the dance troupe was extensive. She would not have worked so hard if she didn't enjoy supporting her husband and the troupe.

"When you see them dancing together, you notice a certain spark. Rufino pulls out the best in anyone with whom he dances, but when he dances with his wife, you see something special."

Rufino is not one to let personal difficulties get him down, Isabel says.

"Even after his horrific traffic accident in Madison, he concentrated on what he *could* do and not on what he could *not* do. When people visited him during the early recovery days, he would talk about them rather than about himself. When pressed, he would say 'Things are doing better'."

Rufino has great strength in dancing and as an educator, Isabel confirms.

"He also has great strength in his religious beliefs. He is very active in his church, St. Albert's, in Madison. His religious convictions are strong in determining how he leads his life and treats his family and friends. The family spends a good amount of time in prayer."

The Piana home was always open. Isabel recalls Rufino and Eppie attending a Christmas decorating party when they had an artificial tree downstairs and a real tree upstairs.

"They helped to decorate both the tree and cookies that we made later. Occasionally, they would stay overnight at our home. They would take Mom's bedroom (Dad had passed by that time), Mom took my bed, I slept in the living room on the couch, and the Licos girls wrapped themselves in quilts and slept on the living room floor. Heidi stayed overnight on one occasion.

"During one evening, she went into the bathroom and, somehow, set off our house alarm. On her next visit, she was very cautious about using the bathroom and pointedly asked if she would set off the alarm. We don't know to this day how she tripped the system."

Nancy Hagan

Nancy Hagan is a nurse manager at Meriter Hospital in Madison. She has known Rufino since he was her Spanish teacher at Waterloo High School.

"He taught me to learn with gusto. Whatever you're going to learn, learn it well and enjoy the process, he would tell me. Put enjoyment into your learning and don't make learning feel like drudgery. With him, education felt so positive. When people ask me what I would do with a million dollars, I answer that I would use it to keep learning so I can continue to give to others. That's what Rufino does for others; he keeps giving for their benefit. His energy is endless."

Rufino was different from other teachers Nancy had in that regard, she recalls. Learning was easy for her, and he gave life to learning during the three years he was her teacher. Instead of asking students simply to acquire knowledge, he put life into learning by making it reality based.

"Spanish was not just a language; it was the language within a culture and its people. I would walk into the class knowing we had something to accomplish each day, but there also would be surprises — some of which Rufino didn't know about. You went with the surprises but stayed on course, and I liked that motion — always moving forward but with wide boundaries. That made the subject so much fun."

Rufino was the first person Nancy met who came from a different culture. Her first impression was that he was alive in a different way.

"Our prior Spanish teacher also was fully engaged and I expected that attitude out of the language. But she was more controlled. Rufino's attitude seemed to be: 'we're going to learn Spanish, have fun doing it, and see where it takes us.' He was happy just being himself as he helped others learn."

Nancy and Rufino at Meriter Hospital – 2003.

Rufino's energies would go into evenings and Saturdays when the class had Spanish Club activities.

"When we had a project requiring us to make tacos, not only did we have to make them, we had to sort them, pack them, deliver them, and account for them. We made a lot of money that way for trips to Spain and elsewhere. We all worked together and had a great deal of fun. It probably was the first experience some families had with tacos. We were used to doing hot dogs and hamburgers. It was always something different with Rufino."

Rufino always seemed sure of himself, sure that education was important and that he had the ability to teach it. He always was comfortable with himself. He also taught students to perform Filipino dances at various activities. Nancy considered herself kind of a klutz until Rufino told her she could dance and then made it so easy and fun that she wanted to be part of every dance activity. She was successful, she insists, because of his prodding.

Rufino also taught CCD for St. Joseph's Catholic Church. Nancy recalls that both at the church and the school he was like a magnet with an energy meter.

"When you're around him, your energy goes up on the meter. I run into him all over the city today because we live on the same side of the town. He seems to be everywhere. He's always the same: energy, happy to see you, and a hug. That's how he is and it's a good feeling for those around him. You wouldn't know from him or Eppie all the physical problems he's had and still is having. He always is positive in his attitude and appearance. When he's down, he seems to get energy from something else. I would like to bottle that quality for myself and others. When he leaves you, some of the energy remains in the air for a time."

Rufino is total outward energy that lights up the room, Nancy says. Eppie is gentle and kind energy, always a smile, always welcoming, more quiet and introspective, always a touch on the arm, always asking about the family.

"Rufino knew how to keep us on task as students. There were days when we would put him to the test. He would let us have fun in class, but he would sternly remind us when we had to come back to our lessons and when that happened, we knew the time for fooling around had ended. He always was pleasant, but you knew when to get back on task.

"If he ever became angry, it was over inequities in the system that put some students or parents at a disadvantage. It wasn't his normal disposition, so we knew when something was bothering or hurting him – and that wasn't often."

Rufino always was interested in his students as whole people and not just as students.

"When he saw something going on that probably wasn't right, he wouldn't criticize, but he would make us think about whether our attitudes and actions were right. He never said we were doing something that was bad, but he set us to thinking about those actions and attitudes. My parents had me on a good path and my interaction with Rufino helped to keep that path enjoyable through his guidance at school.

"He was one of the teachers who was just okay with my being a student. He respected me as a student, knowing that I was growing at my own speed, as opposed to trying to take me somewhere at his speed. It was like having a guardian angel at school. There was an energy around him that was nowhere else in the room."

Dr. Norman Aliga

When Norman and Olive arrived in Madison in 1982, where he began his professional training at the University of Wisconsin, recalls Norman, "we joined an organization where we could continue to express our Filipino heritage through dancing. Rufino was our folk dance leader. He took great interest in this avocation, obviously relishing the opportunity to project what is positive about his origins.

"His entire family, including his in-laws, have been models of this strong Filipino trait. The Licoses received us as if we were old friends, cooking for us, even if we dropped by unannounced. They always were ready to help and they have become known as contacts for Filipinos coming to the Madison area."

Jane Caparroso, Heidi, Olive and Dr. Norman Aliga

"When Rufino does something for you, you know, you see, and you feel that he is giving you a gift of himself, devoid of any expectations in return. Twice he brought Eppie and their girls to the Aliga home in Wheaton, Illinois (140 miles southeast of Madison), to perform native dances at the birthday parties of the Aliga's older two boys.

"Rufino occasionally has been the subject of jealousy and negative treatment by some folks, which he has accepted with quiet humility. Years later, some of those same people have realized the unjustness of their comments and have apologized to him. He has never been a vindictive person.

"Rufino has shown his inner strength in adapting to his adopted country and its culture while not losing his native values. He always looks at the bright side and his outlook on life is contagious to those around him."

Robert J. Fowell

Few people will leave an indelibly positive mark on your life. Bob Fowell says with conviction. "Still fewer will you meet early in life and continue to look up to in later years. I have had such an opportunity in my association with Rufino Licos beginning in the summer between my eighth and ninth grade years at high school.

"During those days, Mom and Dad invited Mr. Licos over for supper several times a week, as did Bill and Joan Brown. We always had a great time; Mom was a wonderful cook and after supper we gathered in the living room to play checkers, a board game, or to just sit and talk. It was particularly the way Mr. Licos both talked and listened to everyone that helped shape my adult life."

"Mr. Licos began to attend our Boy Scout outings shortly after he arrived in Richland Center, and later became an assistant scoutmaster. I remember swimming, hiking, and canoeing with him, but mostly sitting around a campfire swapping tales and telling jokes.

"Mr. Licos was my ninth grade Algebra teacher. His style was most unusual and effective. He taught us to understand algebra in addition to learning the essential rules. He would ask a question and then walk slowly around the room. It was not long before hands would be raised as students eagerly waited to receive his nod to reveal the answer. Mr. Licos was able to teach everyone in the class, not only from the book but from his heart. He instilled great joy in attending his classes, and his students actually looked forward to learning from him.

"I remember the sadness the entire school felt when Mr. Licos left us suddenly to attend his mother's funeral in the Philippines. We weren't certain if he would have a job when he returned, but we learned later that the school board was most gracious in giving him an extended leave to make the trip. No one wanted to see him leave our school system. As much as he did not want to be away from us, he always considered his family the most important element in his life.

"As an adult, I have remained in contact with the Licos family for many years. His influence on me has been positive and continuous. Following in Mr. Licos' footsteps, my time and my family are most precious to me. I also am heavily involved with Scouts, our church, and our community, all as a result of the influence he had on me during my high school years."

Jane Aliga-Caparroso.

When Jane and "Caps" Caparroso need a special kind of help, whether it be heaping doses, just a pat on the back, or words of encouragement, their never-fail, foolproof no-buts-about-it, let's-go-get-'em guy has been Manong Rufino.

Jane and "Caps" Caparroso's wedding

Caps' employer assigned him to Wisconsin in 1998 as an IT consultant, and shipped his belongings to the apartment of his new colleagues Erick Monforte, Allan Rosanes, Peter Swann, and Darwin Rebudiao. Before his luggage made it through the doorway, he was told

Jane and Caps' wedding day. Left to right: Alfonso Aliga, Jr., Alma and Peter Kort, Elenita Aliga, Ernivic "Caps" and Jane Caparroso, Eppi, Raechel, Heidi, Rufino, Neri, Gina, and Elaine Aliga

that the first order of business would be to visit the Licos residence to meet Manong Rufino who was their friend, tennis buddy, confidante, father figure, and cheerleader.

As it turned out, Caps had a special "in" with the Licos family because Jane, Caps' fiancée at that time, was the niece of Rufino's university friend Dr. Norman Aliga.

Neri and godson Jacob Monforte

When Caps' new apartment friends went to work the next day, he was dropped off at Manong Rufino and Manang Eppie's home. Rufino and Eppie immediately asked what they could do to help.

"Need a social security card? What about a driver's license? Want to see the UW campus? We'll take you to the proper government office and drive you around the UW campus.

"You need to go to the post office to send all that mushy stuff to Jane? Hey, those post office guys are all my buddies. Did I tell you about the time that I had a discussion with some people about what letter carriers do, so I went to the post office and asked them to write down all the responsibilities of carriers.

"Need to fetch Wally Abaya at the airport? Need to go to Milwaukee? Shall we buy a tennis racket for you? How about a mah-jongg set? Need to establish credit for Caps, Wally, Aya Ramos, and Rommel Belvis so you can get a new apartment? Put my name down as a co-signor if you need a new car. Here, use my van to carry whatever furniture you buy. And when you're done, we're going to the tennis court!"

"Let's play, you guys!" Whenever Manong said those words, everyone had their tennis gear (or their mah-jongg money) ready within ninety seconds.

Jane followed Caps to Madison in 1999. The second night that they were in their new apartment two miles from the

Licoses, she and Caps realized they had no phone, no bed, no furniture, not even a piano.

"What we did have was Darwin's car and a bad meal that sent them running to the bathroom. Without giving Rufino and Eppie any warning, they drove to their home and asked, 'May we stay here for awhile? We're not feeling well. Oh, and may we use your bathroom right away?'

"Manong and Manang replied, 'Our home is your home.' We felt so much better just sitting at the large round table in their dinette. Since then, Manong and Family have helped us has grow to immense proportions. We're a thousand miles and one time zone away, and yet there's no end to the ways in which they touch us.

The day Jane and Caps left Madison three years ago, they needed to pay one more month of rent at their Village Green complex, but they couldn't find their check book. In the rush of getting their affairs in order for the drive to Connecticut on the East Coast, they had packed their checks in one of the boxes.

"Manong and Manang paid our rent with a smile. They also extended help to anyone whom we brought around. When my 21-year-old sister, who was born in the States but had lived most of her life in the Philippines, wanted to get a social security number during a visit, Manong drove her to the local Social Security office and chatted away with the Spanish-speaking clerk to help the process move quickly.

Godchildren Martha and Allan Rosanes

"When my college friend visited the UW campus, Manong & Manang gladly played tour guide. When Dad and my brother visited Madison and wanted to play tennis while my Mom played mah-jongg, it was Manong and Manang who were at their beck and call for almost eighteen hours each day.

No matter what kind of help anyone needed or wanted, and no matter how far away they were, Manong and Manang were always available, even to chat on the phone, Jane says.

When Caps and Jane were established in New Jersey, I had a dilemma with a student I was tutoring. I decided to confer with a master teacher and I called Manong on a busy December night. He was kind enough to listen and talk for at least twenty minutes, even though it was one of those extremely hectic pre-Christmas nights when he undoubtedly had a busy schedule ferrying one or more of the Licos ladies to or from some kind of Yuletide festivity.

Jet and Elvin Pedro

"Manong and Manang have great intercessory powers. When Mom and my mother-in-law had health concerns and we needed "prayer warriors" to give our families comfort and strength, I was told by each mother not to tell people about their distress. Regardless, I went behind their backs and called Rufino and Eppie. Manong, I said, I'm not supposed to tell anyone but I'm telling you anyway because I know a man like you has a direct line to God.

"While Caps was in the shadow of the Twin Towers on the morning of Sept. 11, 2001, I had no one else to speak with to calm my fears, I was unable to reach him on his cell immediately after the second plane hit. Due to overload of telephone calls around the country, I had immense difficulty reaching anyone, including Caps on his cell phone, and I was extremely worried about him.

"My family members in California were still asleep and did not hear my frantic calls, so I turned again to the Licos family back in Madison for comfort and strength. Hearing Manong and Manang's voices that morning was so reassuring, and when I finally reached Caps a few hours later, I told him that many people were praying for his safety. With Manong and Manang leading the way, I knew Caps had many angels watching over him that morning.

"When Caps finally returned to our home much later that day, one of the first things we said to each other was, Let's move back to Wisconsin!

"We want to move back to Wisconsin because even if we've been away for three years, we feel as though we know the whole town as a result of our connection to the Licoses. It's our home away from home, and Eppie and Rufino, though not our blood, surely are our family."

Aya and Rommel Belvis

Epifania Avecilla Licos

Eppie Avecilla was upstairs when Rufino dropped in to see her mother and her Aunt Marcelina.

"Rufino's downstairs," her mother called to her. "We're playing Scrabble."

"Who cares?" Eppie replied.

Christmas in the 1990s

"I had absolutely no interest in Rufino when I was a teenager. When we met on the street in San Gabriel, I wouldn't even look at him. Often, I'd just turn around. It wasn't that I disliked him, he just didn"t interest me at that time."

One month before Eppie's graduation in nursing from St. Rita Hospital School of Nursing and Midwifery in Manila, the director of nursing at Dauphin Hospital in Dauphin, Manitoba, Canada, wrote to St. Rita's noting that they were in need of ten nurses. Eppie was one of the ten offered the opportunity to emigrate to Canada in her late teens to work as a nurse.

"Being a fresh graduate, I was hesitant to go all the way to Canada because I didn't have any practical experience. Nevertheless, with the encouragement of our school administrator, Dr. Pilar Valdez Albano, I accepted the offer and worked at Dauphin for six years. Then I transferred to the Health Sciences Center (formerly Winnipeg General Hospital) in Winnipeg, Manitoba

When Rufino moved to Wisconsin, his Aunt Marcelina presented him with Eppie's address in Winnipeg, suggesting that he write to her. He did so and they wrote back and forth beginning in 1968, growing closer through their letters. Then Eppie learned from her younger brother Alex that Rufino was engaged to a woman who lived in his home town back in the Philippines.

Upon Alex's suggestion, Eppie ended her letter writing to Rufino and threw away his last letter. For some reason, however, she tore the address off the envelope and tucked it in her wallet. Six years later, she purchased a new wallet. In cleaning out the old wallet, she came across Rufino's address.

Believing he probably was married, she wrote a quick note asking about his career and inquiring about the number of children he must have. Back came the response that he was not married, not engaged, and that he would like to visit her in Winnipeg if she was willing.

"Don't come," she replied, not quite understanding why she did not wish to see him. Shortly afterward, she received a letter from her Aunt Teodora, who com-

Eppie wearing a gown made in the Philippines

mented that her niece now was twenty-nine years old and should be married. Eppie smiled to herself and continued the correspondence with Rufino. Eventually, Rufino wrote that he had waited a long time to marry, thank God, and he was sure Eppie was the woman for him. Eppie replied that he was the man for her and Rufino flew to Winnipeg for their first meeting.

Eppie and lantern made by Rufino for Christmas

As Rufino entered the airport terminal, his eyes met Eppie's and confirmed the growing affection that had developed through months of letter writing. Approaching to within touching distance, they stood quietly gazing at each other for a full minute, then slowly embraced and kissed. Their romance has continued for three decades.

Rufino remained in Winnipeg for one month. Although they knew they were in love, neither fully committed to the other because of the seriousness of marriage. As he left Eppie to return to the United States, Rufino promised he would come back to Canada in three weeks and they would decide what to do.

Three weeks later, Rufino did return and suggest that Eppie join him in Richland Center to learn more about life in the United States. Eppie's culture would not allow her to travel alone with a man, so she asked her roommate to come join them. In those days, a girl did not entertain a man without a parent or a girlfriend in the room. Years later, when Eppie's daughter Heidi dated in

Eppie and Heidi – 2003

the presence of her grandmother, the elder woman sat in the room with the young people. She stated: "time to go home" when she felt the evening should end, and that was the end of the date.

Once back home in Wisconsin, Rufino again declared his love for Eppie and suggested a December wedding. Eppie smiled and agreed that a wedding was in her thoughts. However, she asked, could Rufino wait until July.

"I have to ask for the blessings of my parents," she told him. He replied that he could wait. They went to his church in Richland Center to tell the priest of their intent. While there, Rufino put his hand in his pocket, removed a ring that he had purchased days earlier, and put it on Eppie's finger.

"It was like getting married right there," Eppie

Eppie at home in Madison

says. "I had been in love with him for six years. I couldn't help myself. He was a very nice guy then and he has remained a nice guy through all the years. When we went home to the Philippines to celebrate our first wedding anniversary, one of his sisters-in-law told me I was very lucky to get Rufino. I am always proud of him. My brother told me before the wedding that I was marrying not an ordinary man but a nice man and a professional man.

Following the wedding in Winnipeg, they remained in Canada for three weeks. They then visited friends in Minnesota before settling in Wisconsin.

"All my family speaks well of Rufino. He and my mom have never had a disagreement and she always speaks well of him. That has to be unusual in a marriage."

The marriage coupled deep mutual love with a need to understand and respect the customs and preferences of a partner who had lived thirty years without daily close companionship. Separation seemed inevitable on at least one occasion during the first year of marriage.

One day, Eppie said "no more." They called their parents (who were living with them in Madison at the time) and said they were going to separate.

"For three days and nights we said nothing to each other," Eppie recalls. Then she went to Rufino.

"I will change because I love you and you love me. But please, don't change me overnight. Whatever you see that you don't like, please correct me and I will do my best to change. You are my husband and some day we will have children. I will change for you; just don't make me change all at once."

The fireplace in Madison

In return, Rufino told Eppie that he also would change and that they would learn to compromise. All that took place in the first year of their marriage. Eppie remembers the transition.

"Little by little I changed. My folks noticed the changes and praised me for how I was improving my life. Some things Rufino wanted me to change were very hard for me. We both cried many times. But I changed because our love was deeper than any way of life could harm."

Rufino also learned the art of compromise, and from that time forward, they have been happy and secure in their marriage. The four children are their continuing inspiration.

"We want families everywhere to know how we raised our children," they agree, "in the hope that many others will follow our examples. It's not that our four wonderful girls have always been angels, but they have been good children. They are respectful among older adults as well as their own generation of friends. They have studied hard and well to be successful in their lives. They are aware of the comfort that comes when they open their minds and hearts to God."

In October 1998, Eppie went on disability leave from Meriter Hospital for five months when she injured her right shoulder while she and a nursing assistant lifted a 90-year-old patient scheduled for surgery. Eppie shifted her daily work to the hospital's risk management until she was free of pain, and then returned to her regular assignment in general surgery, orthopedic, urology, and plastic surgery.

Five months later, however, she injured her left shoulder when she assisted another patient who was being prepared for emergency surgery. She was attempting to unlock the patient's bed mechanism when she felt her left hand catch in the locking device. She swung her arm as hard as she could to free herself and heard something crack in her shoulder.

When she developed severe pain fifteen minutes later and noticed that her shoulder was swollen, she went to her doctor and was told to lift no more than thirty pounds until the injury healed. The doctor subsequently restricted her to

Eppie dancing the Igorat – 1988

188

lifting no more than ten pounds. Eppie applied for and received worker's compensation because hospital policy requires nurses to have the capability to lift more than fifty pounds.

"Physical therapy eased my pain over time," Eppie says, "but in spite of the improvement of my shoulder, the hospital would not allow me to return to my regular job until I was cleared by my doctor, the hospital doctor, and the physical therapist. Finally, with the help of God, I passed the lifting test and returned to work in November 2000 after being on disability for almost one year."

Audrey Langer, Eppie's nursing colleague at Meriter for more than twenty years, and Neri's godmother, considers Eppie "a wonderful nurse who is caring and compassionate with her patients. Over the years, I have seen Eppie invent several useful medical equipment items, including an external urinary catheter

Audrey and Atty. Rick Langer

with an adhesive closure, and an ice pack with ties. She came close to receiving patents for both inventions, but others received patents for substantially the same products with slightly different designs."

Audrey also notes that throughout their married life, Eppie and Rufino have "opened their hearts and homes to new members of the Filipino communities in Madison and Milwaukee. They have helped to provide food, housing, clothing, furniture, transportation, and jobs to numerous individuals and families arriving in Wisconsin. Their support and encouragement has been selfless and sustaining to many hardworking Filipino immigrants."

Kathy Dineen, nurse manager, ambulatory surgery, at Meriter Hospital in Madison, and Eppie's supervisor, summarizes Eppie's career by noting that " over the last twenty-five years,

Kathy Dineen

189

you have done much that has influenced many. This truly is an accomplishment of which you can be very proud."

KNOW YOUR MADISONIAN

Couple often act as 'welcome mat'

The Licos family welcomes Filipino immigrants into its home and teaches Americans about the Filipino culture.

By Doug Erickson
Wisconsin State Journal

Rufino Licos said his neighbors sometimes jokingly ask him if he and his wife, Eppie, are running a hotel out of their far East Side home.

Friends liken their residence to sort of the Ellis Island of the Midwest for newly arrived Filipinos. There's always a warm meal, an understanding ear and a welcoming smile there, plus a place to stay a few nights or longer if needed.

"They really care about the Filipinos who migrate here," said Agnes Cammer, a Filipina and longtime Madison community activist. "They are like the welcome mat."

The Licoses and their four daughters not only open their home to others, but they also are ambassadors of the Filipino culture, performing native dances several times a year throughout Wisconsin, including at Milwaukee's Summerfest and the State Fair. As cultural director of the Philippine-American Association of Madison and Neighboring Areas (PAMANA), Rufino Licos organizes presentations that recount the history and customs of the Philippines, an island country in the southwest Pacific Ocean.

The presentations enlighten Americans and keep the culture alive for Filipinos here, said Beth Reyes, a special education teacher at Madison's Lindbergh Elementary School.

"Some of us didn't really have the time to be engaged in cultural performances when we were in the Philippines," she said. "Rufino really knows how to teach that. It's a talent he has."

The family's contributions have gained national attention. In January, they were inducted

cause there are a lot of Filipinos in the Midwest," said Cammer, a founder of PAMANA, which counts about 150 families as members. The Licoses reach out not just to Filipinos, but members of other ethnic groups in the Madison area, she said.

Rufino Licos said the Filipino culture is based on the family — both the nuclear family and the extended family of friends and neighbors. That's why when newcomers move to Madison, he often drives them to job interviews or helps them understand immigration procedures. Some of the newcomers are trying to find permanent jobs here, while others are in the United States temporarily for work contracts or to take college classes, he said.

"We orient them about their life here, what to expect," he said. "We tell them, 'Life here is really not that easy. You have to work here to maintain a living.'"

Rufino Licos, 61, came to the United States 33 years ago from San Gabriel, Philippines. One of his high school teachers had spoken highly of the United States, so, after becoming a teacher himself in the Philippines, he decided to see what this country had to offer. Now retired, he taught high school math in Richland Center, and math, Spanish and English in Waterloo.

Eppie Licos, 56, also grew up in San Gabriel, becoming a nurse. Upon graduation, she was one of 19 nurses selected to begin their careers in Winnipeg, Manitoba. She now is a nurse at Meriter Hospital in Madison.

"The dream of anyone is to come to the United States," she said. "So no matter how busy we are, we try to help newcomers. Even though our house is not big, they can stay as long as they want. And we try to help not only newcomers, but people who already are here."

The couple's living room is a gallery of the family's achievements. There are plaques and certificates awarded the Licoses over the years for their

ANDY MANIS/photo

Rufino and Eppie Licos show some of the photos of Filipinos they have helped over the years. The couple and their four daughters recently were inducted into the Filipino American Hall of Fame in Chicago for their service to the Filipino community.

Profile: Rufino and Eppie Licos

◆ **Jobs:** Rufino is a retired high school teacher who works part-time in security at the Dane County Regional Airport. Eppie is a nurse at Meriter Hospital.

◆ **Ages:** Rufino is 61; Eppie, 56.

◆ **Family:** Four daughters: Heidi, 21, Regina, 20, Neri, 18, and Raechel, 15

◆ **The person I admire most:** Former Gov. Tommy Thompson because of his dedication to the people of the state of Wisconsin. Due to this, he is again selected to serve the people of the United States. (Rufino and Eppie)

◆ **I wish I had more time for:**

Teaching. I love to listen to and to help the youth of today to prepare them to be successful in their futures. (Rufino)

◆ I've always envied people who can: Reach higher than I can. (Rufino)

◆ Over the years, I've become: More helpful to people in need. (Rufino and Eppie)

◆ If I could convince people of one thing, it would be: To respect one another no matter who or what they are. (Rufino and Eppie)

◆ The accomplishment I am most proud of is: The help that I have rendered to people and the way I brought up my four girls to be respectful and helpful to others. (Rufino and Eppie)

"They are our world," Rufino Licos said of his daughters, ages 15 to 21. The six family members perform as "The Philippine Dance Troupe of Madison and the Licos Girls."

Eppie's parents, Agueda, 89, and Caridad, 87, also live with the family. Caridad often sews

on the board of directors of the Black Hawk Council of Girl Scouts, and he's a member of Knights of Columbus. The family attends St. Albert the Great Catholic Church in Sun Prairie.

The Licoses said that when their daughters are grown, they hope to one day return to the Philippines as volunteers.